The Grace Abbott Reader

GRACE ABBOTT

The Grace Abbott Reader

Edited by John Sorensen *with* Judith Sealander

UNIVERSITY OF NEBRASKA PRESS · LINCOLN & LONDON

We offer our deepest gratitude to the
Edith Abbott Memorial Library for
their ongoing support of the Abbott
Sisters Project and for their invaluable
help in honoring the living legacy of
Grace and Edith Abbott.

Acknowledgments for the use of
copyrighted material appear on
pages 107–9, which constitute an
extension of the copyright page.

Library of Congress Cataloging-
in-Publication Data
Abbott, Grace, 1878–1939.
The Grace Abbott reader /
Grace Abbott ; edited by John
Sorensen with Judith Sealander.
p. cm.
Includes bibliographical
references and index.
ISBN 978-0-8032-1590-0
(pbk. : alk. paper)
1. Abbott, Grace, 1878–1939.
2. Abbott, Edith, 1876–1957.
3. Women social reformers—
United States—Biography.
4. Women social workers—
United States—Biography.
5. Feminists—United States.
6. Social justice. I. Sorensen,
John, 1958– . II. Sealander,
Judith. III. Title.
HQ1413.A33A3 2008
361.92'273–dc22
[B]
2008008157

Set in New Baskerville by Kim Essman.

Some women and some men wonder why change in the position of woman has been desired. Repeatedly they ask, "Why should anyone choose the 'strenuous life'? Why seek a part in the struggle to end the injustice and ugliness of our modern life?"

They are the lotus-eaters, who prefer to live in a gray twilight in which there is neither victory nor defeat. It is impossible for them to understand: that to have had a part in the struggle—to have done what one could—is in itself the reward of effort and the comfort in defeat.

—GRACE ABBOTT, 1930

Contents

Introduction

Justice for all children is the high ideal in a democracy.

—GRACE ABBOTT

Grace Abbott led a lifelong fight for justice on behalf of those least able to claim justice for themselves—a cause that she saw as crucial to a larger "struggle for fundamental change" within society as a whole. This belief was central to Abbott's career as a reformer and government leader—from her early days at Jane Addams's Hull House settlement, through her years as director of Chicago's Immigrants' Protective League, and culminating in her influential tenure as chief of the U.S. Children's Bureau in Washington DC.

In addition to her lasting achievements for children and immigrants, Abbott also took an important part in the struggle to establish women's role in government, including her breakthrough accomplishments as the first person sent to represent the United States on a League of Nations committee and as the first woman in American history nominated for a presidential cabinet post.

Throughout her impressive career, Abbott held a deep belief in the power of well-crafted words, as this volume makes clear. She published extensively, her name becoming familiar to readers of, on the one hand, scholarly journals such as the *Social Service Review* or the *American Journal of Sociology* and, on the other, to the much larger audiences available to her as a columnist for the *Chicago*

Evening Post and through articles for *Parents* and other popular magazines. Abbott's books and articles on the educational needs of immigrants, the history of child labor law, the casework responsibilities of juvenile courts, and public-relief policy became standard texts valued by succeeding generations of social workers and public-policy analysts.

But if Abbott saw writing as a vital tool for reform, she also appreciated the unique powers of the spoken word and visual images for communicating ideas, and she embraced her era's newest technologies from radio to motion pictures. She was, with her weekly NBC radio series, one of the first American women regularly broadcasting to large national audiences over the airwaves and was an avid proponent of the educational applications of lantern slides and movies. As Abbott explained, her goal at the Children's Bureau was not just to speak to experts and specialists but "to reach the public"—by whatever means worked best for them. It was this pragmatic sense of "equalitarianism" that led Abbott to such diverse honors as receiving the Gold Medal of the National Institute of Social Sciences, while also being named one of the "Twelve Greatest Living American Women" in a nationwide poll conducted by *Good Housekeeping* magazine—both in the same year!

This collection of Abbott's speeches and essays, divided into sections based on her work for immigrants, children, and women, allows easy access to a group of lively but until now unpublished archival or out-of-print sources. These excerpts illuminate the life and thoughts of an early-twentieth-century American who deserves recognition, and they focus attention on a network of reformers who were joined together by interconnected social welfare crusades. The essays also comprise a series of first-hand explanations of early-twentieth-century progressivism, and they serve as case studies on the impact of the growth of the federal government in the early twentieth century, when ideas about private versus public responsibilities were uniquely in flux. Finally, they act as a measuring stick by which to judge the possibilities of progress.

Appropriately, Abbott's older sister, Edith Abbott, provides introductions to two of this volume's sections of essays. Grace Abbott made numerous lifelong alliances with fellow female reformers, but her first and most important was the bond she forged with her sister. Indeed "partnership" inadequately describes a relationship that included shared living quarters, joint research and writing, and fiercely mutual admiration. The Abbott sisters of Grand Island, Nebraska, possessed reformers' zeal as a family birthright. Their mother, Lizzie, a Quaker and ardent abolitionist, was an early feminist. Her girls, Grace once wryly explained, were born believing in the cause of women's rights.

Among those rights was equal opportunity for education. Both Edith and Grace, first trained as schoolteachers, soon sought additional schooling at the University of Chicago. Founded in 1891 with bequests made by John D. Rockefeller Sr., the university quickly became a major force in American higher education. When Edith Abbott arrived in Chicago in 1903, with Grace soon to follow, the city was a boomtown, and the university was its intellectual center, a champion of new ideas and new disciplines—particularly sociology, social work, anthropology, and psychology.

Their search for higher education made the Abbott sisters members of a growing company of white, middle-class women who enthusiastically embraced the chances an urbanizing, professionalizing society offered for a life outside the confines of the home. By 1900 more than eighty-five thousand of these women were students at over one thousand colleges; more than a million female graduates were already employed in white-collar jobs as teachers, librarians, office staff, nurses, and social workers.

While many of this first group of highly educated American women attended gender-segregated institutions, Grace and Edith Abbott chose coeducation. The early-twentieth-century Midwest was notable for its number of colleges and universities that allowed women and men to study together. Therefore, the world of reform this volume illuminates was not exclusively a female one. Not only did Grace

Abbott study with men, and along with them help create the new professional fields of social work and public welfare administration, she also lived with them at Chicago's Hull House, the famous Halsted Street settlement begun by Jane Addams in 1889, as part of what Edith Abbott affectionately called "a very argumentative family group."

Grace Abbott, born a decade after the end of the Civil War in 1878, belonged to a generation of women that was the least likely to wed in all of American history. Certainly the carnage of the war reduced the availability of potential husbands; nonetheless, that fact alone cannot explain the significant percentage of female never-marrieds in the United States at the turn of the century. The lure of nondomestic possibilities was powerful, and college graduates dominated the ranks of single women. Included among them were Grace and Edith Abbott as well as Jane Addams, Ellen Starr, Sophonisba Breckinridge, and Julia Lathrop—all close friends, Hull House residents, and fellow advocates of immigrants', children's, and women's rights.

Grace Abbott, then, typified women's emergence into public life at the turn of the century. A professional career and marriage, as she notes in these pages, rarely mixed. However, Grace Abbott's contacts always reached beyond exclusively female circles. If women numbered among her allies, so, too, did men: English reformer Sidney Webb, prominent legal scholar Roscoe Pound, and New Deal insider Harry Hopkins.

What bound them all together was a shared status as progressives (reformers who gave their name to the era from 1870 to 1920). A movement—not a political party—progressivism demanded both social and political change. And while progressives sheltered under an umbrella belief that America could be a better place for all, they differed on many specifics. Some thought trade unions should be discouraged. Others, with whom Grace Abbott cooperated, wanted such organizations to thrive at home and internationally. Some were pacifists, as was Grace. Others ardently advocated American use of force abroad, as did Theodore Roosevelt. The causes embraced by progressives spanned a huge gamut including advocacy of special juvenile courts, demands for improvements in urban housing and sanitation, crusades to purify food and ban alcohol, and efforts to regulate corporations. No single person embodied all causes or all aspects of progressivism; nor did progressives reach consensus on even one cause. Grace Abbott's acceptance in 1908 of a position as the first director of Chicago's Immigrants' Protective League drew her quickly into an issue about which debate was notably fierce—the rights of immigrants.

At the height of the progressive era, between 1890 and the outbreak of World War I, more than fifteen million newcomers arrived in the United States. Though the proportion of immigrants was not remarkably different from earlier decades (about 16 percent of the total population), the sources of immigration were. Before 1880 most had come from northern Europe, particularly the British Isles, Germany, and Ireland. By the beginning of the twentieth century, more than eight out of ten came from southern and eastern Europe. They were Italians, Greeks, Hungarians, Russians, and Poles. They were not Protestants, not English speakers, and not, many said, as easily assimilable as the earlier "Anglo-Saxons" had been.

Progressivism was a crusade spurred by faith in progress—and by fear. Optimists enthusiastically saw possibilities for social betterment. Pessimists demanded change, lest class wars and ethnic divisions shatter the nation. Many progressives expressed both emotions, but Grace Abbott clearly belonged to the optimists, and her writings on immigration in this volume reflect that.

Immigrants, Abbott felt, needed to be protected from fraud and exploitation. They needed practical warnings about abusive employment agencies and clear guidance about licenses for work in trades. They didn't need to be "molded" after "some approved American pattern" or be put in a room and told about "American ideals." And her fellow countrymen need not feel that the use of any other language was a menace to standard English. Moreover,

Abbott, well trained in the emerging rules of sociology and social welfare work at the University of Chicago, was a fervent advocate of scientific investigation and on-site fieldwork. As Chicago filled with hundreds of thousands of immigrant girls from Poland, Russia, Hungary, and Croatia, Abbott was not content to accept hearsay. Instead, in 1911 she traveled alone to eastern Europe to collect data for *The Immigrant and the Community*. Published in 1917, the book (excerpted in this volume) was the first to gain Abbott widespread national attention. *The Immigrant and the Community* provided a nuanced portrait of Chicago's newcomers—and a ringing challenge to "the stupid race prejudices" of native-born Americans.

The challenge was repudiated. In 1924, the National Origins Act embraced fears about post-1880 immigration instead of Abbott's confidence that great ethnic diversity was a source of America's strength. Through the 1960s America's immigration policy severely restricted the number of new arrivals, which was governed by a quota system that favored peoples of northern-European background.

By 1924 Abbott had refocused her energies, left Chicago for Washington, and embraced another progressive cause: children's rights. In 1917 the first director of the United States Children's Bureau, Julia Lathrop, convinced her good friend and fellow Chicagoan to accept an appointment as head of the agency's newly created Child Labor Division. In 1921 Abbott succeeded Lathrop as the bureau's second director. The Children's Bureau, established by Congress in 1912, was itself a progressive victory, reflective of the fact that the desire to improve conditions for children united many in the movement.

The writings in this volume illustrate another progressive trait: the embracement of expanded federal regulatory authority. Even during its period of greatest influence at the height of the New Deal, the Children's Bureau remained small. Between 1917 and 1933, when an ailing Grace Abbott resigned to teach in the University of Chicago's Graduate School of Social Service Administration, the bureau rarely had as many as two hundred employees. Nonetheless, it prophesied the emergence of a more powerful federal government.

Indeed, the excerpts included here implicitly downplay the importance of that change. Abbott quite sincerely thought that all reasonable people should support universal programs of health insurance for children and standardized national codes of child labor. Healthcare, she indignantly wrote, was not to be considered the same as "rugs or motor cars"—with the rich granted higher quality simply because they were able to afford it. The only people who opposed a federal constitutional amendment regulating child labor were those who ". . . were indifferent to the object for which federal aid is sought [or] . . . unfortunately for the children, . . . [those who] like the crazy patchwork quilt of state laws which so unequally protects American children." Not even all progressives agreed with such ideas, which could fairly be called revolutionary, though Abbott never referred to them as such.

The proposed Twentieth Amendment to the U.S. Constitution, passed by Congress in 1924 but never ratified, was the product of standardizers' frustration. Granting the federal government authority to limit, regulate, and prohibit the labor of all persons under age eighteen, it embodied a reform agenda far ahead of even most official state rules for child labor, which generally held the upper limit of childhood at age sixteen. Even federal occupational censuses usually listed all workers over that age as adults. And most early-twentieth-century Americans applauded full-time work after age fourteen.

The so-called Child Labor Amendment was a response to Supreme Court rebuffs. In 1917 Abbott came to Washington as head of the new Children's Bureau division established to administer the Keating-Owen Law. Passed in 1916, Keating-Owen closed interstate commerce to the products of "oppressive" child labor; these "products" were defined in the bill as anything produced in a quarry or mine that employed children under age sixteen or anything produced in a factory that used child workers under age fourteen. When the U.S. Supreme Court declared the act unconstitutional, angry supporters immediately reintroduced it as Title XII, an amendment to the Revenue Act of 1918. Referred to by Abbott and almost everybody else as "the Child Labor Tax Act," the amendment sought to kill the same bird with a different stone. If the federal government could not control child labor through the U.S. Congress's power to oversee interstate trade, then it could tax it to death. Title XII imposed a 10 percent federal tax on the annual net profits of any industry that employed underage workers, using exactly the same definitions employed by Keating-Owen. The Supreme Court, which had declared Keating-Owen an unconstitutional misuse of the Commerce Clause, promptly damned Title XII as an equally unconstitutional "privilege" tax. Taxes, it decreed, should be levied for fiscal, not social, purposes.

Furious advocates of federalized standards for child labor campaigned for a constitutional amendment, which the Supreme Court could not thwart. However, both Keating-Owen and the Child Labor Tax Act reflected national preoccupations with larger problems caused by the United States' entrance into World War I, rather than national support for centralized control of child labor law. At a time when its attention was focused on mobilization, a distracted U.S. Congress passed both bills with little debate. Each, however, was a hollow victory, though Grace and Edith Abbott thought otherwise. Neither made any mention of street selling, domestic service, or seasonal agricultural labor—the occupations of the vast majority of young laborers. At best, each covered about 5 percent of all child workers. Keating-Owen and the Child Labor Tax Act were easy concessions for national politicians to make to a vocal, well-organized, anti–child labor coalition.

The proposed Twentieth Amendment was a different matter. Passed by a U.S. Congress warned by prominent suffragists that millions of just-enfranchised female voters wanted national child labor restrictions, the Child Labor Amendment soon floundered. In 1924, within months of the amendment's passage, Massachusetts held a popular referendum on the proposal. The defeat at the polls was so overwhelming that amendment supporters never again tried to submit the measure to the will of a general electorate.

If the Child Labor Amendment never generated widespread grass-roots support, neither did the "Maternity and Infancy Revolution" embodied in the Sheppard-Towner Maternity and Infancy Protection Act, which was, like Keating-Owen and the Child Labor Tax Act, a federal bill administered by the Children's Bureau. Sheppard-Towner provided federal matching funds to states, enabling them to set up well-baby and parent education programs. During its seven-year lifetime between 1921 and 1928, it focused on "child health conferences," where trained nurses instructed young mothers about the proper care of newborns and toddlers.

Grace and Edith Abbott were right: Sheppard-Towner's "nurse-teachers" dispensed all kinds of useful advice at a modest administrative cost. However, like federal control of child labor, federal involvement with health care was an idea ahead of its time, especially as politicians lost any fear of the fabled women's vote and realized that the millions of new voters given access to the polls by the Nineteenth Amendment did not operate as a bloc. Women were not uniformly in favor of children's federalized health care reform—or anything else. Although Grace Abbott thought all reasonable Americans should support the Children's Bureau's programs, millions thought that children's work and health were not proper concerns of Washington-based bureaucracies. The Catholic Church raised alarms about unnecessary government interference, as did the new profession of pediatrics, worried that Sheppard-Towner nurses might promote the Children's Bureau message that breast milk provided the simplest and most effective nourishment for newborns. The fledgling specialty, at the bottom of the medical pecking order, strongly advocated the superiority of bottle feeding, with physicians, of course, in charge of recipes for formula.

The Children's Bureau was right: breastfeeding was best. But truth rarely trumps politics, especially the politics of emotion that childhood generates. Was Abbott's agency right about other issues? Even in the early twenty-first century that question spurs debate. Like many other progressives Abbott initially saw Supreme Court resistance to federal regulation of child labor as a blessing in disguise. Surely, she thought, the backward thinking of a few old jurists would stimulate citizens around the country to demand a constitutional amendment. Nothing of the sort happened. Supporters of the Sheppard-Towner act could not win renewal of enabling legislation, and the program died. Even a stalwart reformer such as New York's Governor Al Smith fretted that health care was not an appropriate federal function. Politicians, initially cowed by the specter of millions of new women voters tossing them out of office, soon relaxed. Lizzie Abbott dreamed of the power of female suffrage. Grace and Edith proudly marched for the vote. All of the Abbotts thought that the moral strength of female outrage at the ballot box could quickly change America. It did not. In fact, the sound that notably marked American politics by the end of the twentieth century was that of silence as women and men increasingly avoided the polls. The influence of political parties shrank, while that of influence-groups mushroomed. And fewer Americans thought government bureaucracies positively influenced the greater good.

Grace Abbott, in contrast, was a true believer, convinced that government action could solve problems, not worsen them. The Children's Bureau reached the apex of its influence during Abbott's lifetime, as she worked unceasingly to make it a model of the benefits that well-trained, scientifically minded public servants could bring to society. Even after her retirement from government, she stayed in close touch with New Deal allies and frequently returned to the Capitol as an expert witness. Her passionate testimony helped convince Congress to include Title IV, the Aid to Dependent Children Program (ADC), in the historic Social Security Act of 1935.

Social Security greatly expanded the federal government's role as a social policy maker. ADC embodied the kind of federal-state cost sharing that Congress had repudiated when it refused to renew the Sheppard-Towner Maternity and Infancy Protection Act. Nonetheless, the former gradually became a government program that millions, including millions of recipients, loved to hate.

Without Abbott, the Children's Bureau declined. By 1947 its chief no longer reported directly to the Secretary of Labor. As federal bureaucracy mushroomed, the Department of Labor shriveled. By the early 1950s the department had lost over half of its agencies and bureaus to other units of government. The Children's Bureau became a division within the Federal Security Administration, a non-Cabinet level agency. Then, after another round of major re-organizations during the Nixon era, it ended up as a shadow of its former self within the Department of Health, Education, and Welfare. Although the number of federal offices concerned with child welfare metastasized, cacophony, rather than clear leadership, characterized late-twentieth-century federal children's policy.

These pages remind us of a very different, more innocent age. They also, finally, provide a means by which to assess the nature of progress and the realities of social change. Though the phrase "government servant" is still commonly used, how many people accept it as did Grace Abbott? From her girlhood to her death, Abbott was a pioneer—literally and figuratively. Her boldness made enemies. But even her harshest opponents never dared to call her "venal." No one thought her capable of accepting a bribe. She wasn't.

It is worth remembering that Abbott thought government work was a higher calling. She wanted to use state and federal legislatures as agents of social change and advocates for the weak. She did not accompany the phrase "Washington bureaucracy" with a disillusioned shrug. Even when she was the highest ranking female administrator in the federal government while serving as director of the U.S. Children's Bureau, she lived modestly. She returned to private life as a college professor. She never used her wealth of Washington contacts to financially enrich herself. She did not use her middle-class status or her elite university graduate degree as protective shields behind which comfortably to ignore "the terrors" life brought to those less fortunate. She wanted the emerging fields of social work and public welfare administration to serve as bridges for any in America who were left behind. She was, as Secretary of

Labor Frances Perkins notes here in a tribute, an "equalitarian." Abbott did not see herself as innately superior to the Galician peasant drawn in confusion and loneliness to Chicago's tawdry dance halls. She did not see herself as socially superior to anyone, and those who provoked her acidic pen were far more likely to ride in "handsome limousines" than in the other humble vehicles that caused "the Washington traffic jam." What does it say about us that such a life might now be dismissed as overly naive?

Today many more people accept ideas that Grace Abbott embraced ahead of their time: cost-sharing partnerships between different levels of government and expanded public responsibilities for social welfare. These writings reflect that, but they also illustrate other stubborn realities that Grace Abbott herself acknowledged.

Many in the Washington traffic jam set their sites on meeting personally with a member of Congress. And, as Abbott notes in these pages, "[Congressmen] are really just as fond of children as I am. They are fond of their own children and their friends' children, but they are usually not familiar with what is happening to many American children, and they often lack the imagination to translate the facts and figures which are presented to them in terms of actual children."

Decades after Abbott's death, America still mirrors the Congressmen who frustrated her. Talk about the rights of children is common. Few today would see a federal program that attempted to teach parents about good care for infants as revolutionary. Few would find that it crossed a dangerous line toward too much centralized government, especially if the funds were meager and the individual states were still largely in control. But a society far more comfortable with ideas about public regulation of all aspects of childhood is still one which, like Abbott's Congressmen, lacks imagination and will. We remain a society of people who love our own children and ignore the suffering of other people's children. We demand that no child be left behind, but leave plenty of children behind. Medicare, begun in 1965, was our first foray into nationally subsidized health care for a designated group defined by age. It was designated for the old, not the young. We loudly proclaim that children should be protected first, but have allowed children to replace the elderly as the country's most impoverished.

We still talk about immigrants as potentially unassimilable threats to American jobs and ethical standards, with as little concrete evidence as those who made similar charges a century ago. And, finally, almost a century after the passage of the Nineteenth Amendment, ambiguity still marks social attitudes about proper roles for women. Writing in 1933, Grace Abbott recalled a psychologist "who tells us that women [who] have proven their capacity in literature, in science, in art, in the professions, or in social services are not happy. They may imagine that they are, but he knows that they cannot be. . . . Moreover, someone is sure to suggest that the explanation of unhappy man is unhappy woman."

Grace Abbott belonged to the first cohort of college women that faced hard choices between marriage and childbearing or a satisfying professional career. In part "to prove their capacity" in the social sciences, the Abbott sisters remained single. Such early-twentieth-century dilemmas have significantly diminished. Most professional women today are married with children. But have we truly gained the kind of cultural confidence Grace Abbott wanted—to judge talent for talent alone, free of gendered expectations?

This collection of Grace Abbott's writings allows readers to reimage past struggles and reassess present ones. Her joyful, witty, sometimes exasperated prose reaffirms the fact that being part of the struggle enhances humanity. Everyone deserves a "ticket of general admission" to the "fairgrounds" of American public life. No one should be "locked out"—by gender, by ethnicity, or by social prejudice. And how much worse, Grace Abbott also reminds us, it is "to be locked in" to an intellectually gated life of indifference to others.

Edith Abbott and "A Sister's Memories"

Edith Abbott (1876–1957) was the elder sister and lifelong comrade and professional colleague of Grace Abbott. She was also Grace Abbott's primary biographer (and occasional Boswell) and the source of much information and material in this book. For these reasons and many more, it would be quite inappropriate, if not utterly impossible, to tell Grace's story without also telling something of Edith's. Accordingly, it seems useful and necessary to take a moment to introduce this essential character in our story.

Edith Abbott was among the most important Americans who were involved in the establishment of social work as a profession—requiring not merely the "good intentions" of its practitioners, but a scrupulous intellectual education and rigorous practical training.

Edith Abbott's first book, the influential *Women in Industry*, was published in 1910, around the same time that she joined the faculty of the Chicago School of Civics and Philanthropy. She was a key figure in the 1920 effort to move this institution of social work training to the University of Chicago, where it was renamed the School of Social Service Administration. Abbott thereby led the ssa, as it was known, to become one of the first programs of social work—perhaps the very first—at a prominent U.S. university. She became dean of the school in 1924, and was the first woman in U.S. history to become the dean of a major American university graduate school.

For many years and through the Great Depression, Edith Abbott worked closely with her sister to combat a wide array of social ills, from the mistreatment of immigrants to the abuses of child labor. The Abbott sisters formed a complementary team with each providing an invaluable and unique service: one more theoretical, the other more pragmatic. As Edith Abbott put it, "I could assemble the facts and write the report, but Grace had the gift of applying the proper legislative remedy."

Edith Abbott continued to publish important books on immigration, the tenements of Chicago, American pioneers in social welfare, and the philosophy of social welfare education. She was the cofounder in 1927 of the renowned publication *Social Service Review* and was also its longtime editor; she was named president of the American Association of Schools of Social Work from 1925 to 1927; she was appointed to the Wickersham Commission (National Committee on Law Enforcement and Observance) in the late 1920s; and she was the president of the National Conference of Social Work in 1937.

In 1942 Edith Abbott retired from her position as dean of the School of Social Service Administration. She served as dean emeritus and continued teaching until 1952, when she returned to her hometown of Grand Island, Nebraska, where the city library was later named in her honor.

At the time of Edith Abbott's death in 1957, Wayne McMillen of *Social Service Review* wrote, "History will include her name among the handful of leaders who have made enduring contributions to the field of education. Social work has now taken its place as an established profession. She, more than any other one person, gave direction to the education required for that profession. Posterity will not forget achievements such as these."

§

In her later years, Edith Abbott undertook to write a memoir of Grace Abbott's life that was to be titled "A Sister's Memories." Brief selections from the work (for which Edith Abbott left behind over a thousand pages of detailed notes) were issued in *Social Service Review*, but the final manuscript remained uncompleted at the time of her death. It is this unpublished memoir that forms the basis for the following timeline of Grace Abbott's life, and from which two excerpts were drawn for the introductions to parts 1 and 2 of this volume.

Edith Abbott strongly believed that her sister's childhood experiences in Nebraska were of vital importance to any real understanding of Grace Abbott's later career and achievements. Accordingly, she began her memoir with an extended section entitled "A Prairie Childhood" (published posthumously in *Great Plains Quarterly*). This lovely chronicle provides a series of engaging sketches of the Abbott sisters' mother, father, and hometown, all of which played crucial roles in the sisters' development and lives. I have followed Edith Abbott's lead in this matter, and am herewith including (as a preface to the following biographical timeline) a few very brief passages from "A Prairie Childhood," so that the reader may gain a sense of this essential family and hometown background and upbringing.

A Prairie Childhood

"Grace and I always agreed that our most cherished memories were those of our prairie childhood. . . . In the quiet life of an early Western town, family stories and family traditions were important in the lives of children, and our parents' tales seemed to belong to the history of the country and to be part of the great American traditions."

O. A. Abbott

"Two of Father's great-great-grandfathers had been in the Colonial Wars, and one of his grandfathers in the Revolutionary War. . . . Father was the first lawyer in our part of [Nebraska] and the only lawyer in our county in the early years. He drew up the first charter for the city of Grand Island [and was] the state's first Lieutenant Governor. . . . How he loved the law and politics!"

Elizabeth Griffin Abbott

"We knew the story of Mother's Quaker family, the Gardners—how
. . . they believed earnestly in the great crusade for women's rights.
Grace used to say that [thanks to Mother] she was born believing
in women's rights, and certainly, from the earliest days, woman's
suffrage was part of our childhood. 'I was always a suffragist, and
even if you are little girls, you can be suffragists, too, because it is
right and just,' was the teaching in our home."

Grand Island, Nebraska

"We were born in Grand Island, one of the oldest Nebraska towns,
less than a mile from the Overland Trail. Grace used to say that a
small Western town was the most honestly democratic place in the
world. There were no people who were rich, and the poor we all
knew as individuals. They were people who had had one misfortune
or another, people whom we should try to help."

A Daughter of the Pioneers

"To the end of her life my sister Grace was a daughter of the pioneers, with the courage, enthusiasm, and vigorous 'dash' of the
pioneer who is able to accept temporary defeat in the confident
belief in ultimate victory, even when the odds on the other side are
very great. For her the light never failed, and she always saw hope
in the long future."

Grace Abbott

A Biographical Timeline

1842 *Sept. 9*

Grace's father, Othman Ali Abbott, is born in Hartley, Canada; the family later moves to DeKalb County, Illinois

1845 *Jan. 20*

Grace's mother, Elizabeth Meleta Griffin, is born in DeKalb County, Illinois; Elizabeth's father soon dies, and she is raised by her mother's Quaker family, the Gardners

1850s–60s

The Gardners keep a station on the Underground Railroad, helping escaped slaves

1861–65

Othman fights for the Union Army in the U.S. Civil War and studies law

1867 *spring*

Othman is admitted to the bar. He arrives in Grand Island, Nebraska, in a covered wagon and builds the first law office in town

1868

Elizabeth graduates from Rockford College

1868–73

Elizabeth works as a teacher and principal in Iowa

1871

Othman participates as a member of the Nebraska Constitutional Convention

1872

Othman serves in the Nebraska State Senate

1873 *Feb. 9*

Othman and Elizabeth marry

1875

Othman helps to frame the Nebraska constitution

1876 *Sept. 26*

Edith Abbott is born

Othman is elected as the first lieutenant governor of Nebraska

1878 *autumn*

Elizabeth organizes the "Relief Club" in Grand Island

1878 *Nov. 17*

Grace Abbott is born in Grand Island, Nebraska

1882

Meets Susan B. Anthony, who is visiting Grand Island for suffrage work and stays in the Abbott home

Elizabeth works on the Nebraska Suffrage campaign

The suffrage bill fails to pass

Elizabeth persuades the Grand Island Women's Suffrage Society to donate treasury to the founding of the Grand Island public library

1884

The new Abbott home is built across from the County Court House

1886

Elizabeth is appointed by the governor as a delegate to the National Conference of Charities and Corrections (St. Paul, Minnesota)

1893

Grace takes a trip to the Chicago World's Fair with her sister, Edith

1895

Graduates from Grand Island High School

1898

Graduates from Grand Island College

1899 *spring*

Contracts typhoid fever while teaching at the high school in Broken Bow, Nebraska

1899–1907

Takes over her sister Edith's teaching position at Grand Island Senior High

Teaches history and becomes the girls' basketball coach and theater director

Organizes a local women's discussion group

1902–3

Pursues graduate work at the University of Nebraska

1903 *April 27*

Elizabeth helps bring President Theodore Roosevelt to Grand Island for the groundbreaking of the town's new Carnegie Library

1904

Grace takes a trip with friends to Pike's Peak in Colorado

1906

Graduates from the University of Nebraska

Befriends Ruth Bryan, daughter of William Jennings Bryan, with whom she acts in amateur theatricals; Grace even appears in one performance wearing William Jennings Bryan's clothes

Summer

Attends summer school at the University of Chicago

1906–7

Completes her final year teaching at Grand Island Senior High

1907

Attends the University of Chicago, studying law and political science

Writes her thesis entitled "Married Women's Property Rights"

1908

Works with the Juvenile Protection League, which was her first Chicago job; she quits school to live at Hull House Social Settlement and become Director of the Immigrants' Protective League

Works on the Rudovitz case regarding a political refugee from Russia

Battles with employment agencies

1908–17

Serves as director of the Immigrants' Protective League in Chicago

1909

Attends the National Conference of Charities and Corrections with Jane Addams

Prepares a report for the Committee on Immigration with Jane Addams

Works to protect immigrant savings and secures changes in banking laws

1909–10

Writes "Within the City Gates," weekly articles for the *Chicago Evening Post*

1910

Works with the Women's Trade Union League regarding the eight-hour work day

Makes a plan for a domestic immigration policy

1911

Travels to Central Europe (Hungary, Croatia, Galicia, etc.) to study the working and living conditions of emigrants

1912

Grace's testimony to Congress persuades President Taft to veto the immigration "Literacy Test"

1913

Works with the women's suffrage movement in Illinois

1913–14

Appointed and serves as secretary of the Massachusetts Immigration Commission while on leave from the Immigrants' Protective League

1914

Returns to Hull House

1914–15

Serves on the Mayor's Commission on Unemployment in Chicago

1915

Chairs the Special Committee on Penal and Correctional Institutions

Serves as a delegate to the Women's Peace Conference at the Hague with Jane Addams

1916

Organizes and chairs the Conference of Oppressed Nationalities in Washington DC

1917

Named director of the Child Labor Division of the Children's Bureau

Moves to Washington DC

Writes *The Immigrant and the Community*

1918

Asked by President Wilson to serve as secretary to the White House Conference on Child Welfare

Serves as a consultant to the War Labor Policies Board

1919

Represents the Children's Bureau at the London Conference, which helps plan the first International Labor Conference

Grace travels to Paris and Brussels for the Children's Year Conferences

1919–21

Serves as Executive Secretary of the Illinois Immigration Commission where she investigates immigrant conditions in coal-mining districts and works on the adult-education and compulsory education law for immigrant children

Returns to Hull House

Considers running for political office in Nebraska

1920

Chairs the Child Labor section of the Illinois State Children's Commission

1921

Reorganizes the Immigrants' Protective League after the Illinois governor vetoes appropriation for the Illinois Immigration Commission

August

Named Chief of the U.S. Children's Bureau by President Harding

Moves to Washington DC

1921–34

Serves as Chief of the U.S. Children's Bureau where she works extensively concerning child labor, healthcare for women and children, and education

Hosts the NBC radio series *Your Child*, produces motion pictures, and publishes literature, all regarding children's issues

Works for the "Children's Amendment" to the U.S. Constitution
to regulate child labor

1922

Put in charge of administration of the Sheppard-Towner
Maternity and Infancy Act, which is the first system of federal aid
for social welfare in the United States and lasts until 1929
Appointed by President Harding as U.S. Representative to the
League of Nations Advisory Commission on Traffic in Women
and Children; a worldwide inquiry into traffic is made by the
League at her suggestion

1924

Named president of the National Conference of Social Workers
in Toronto
Helps write the "Declaration of the Rights of the Child" with
the League of Nations Committee

1927

Goes to Honolulu for a meeting of the Institute of Pacific
Relations
Suffers from tuberculosis

1928

Becomes seriously ill and spends time recovering in
Colorado

1929

Fights with President Hoover over the upcoming White House
Child Welfare Conference

1930

Fights to preserve the Children's Bureau at the White House
Conference of 1930

August

Attends the Geneva meeting regarding Traffic of Women and
Children in the Orient
Nationwide campaign for Grace to become the Secretary of
Labor in President Hoover's Cabinet; she is the first woman in
U.S. history to be nominated for a presidential cabinet post

1931

Awarded the National Institute of Social Sciences Gold Medal

Named one of "America's Twelve Most Distinguished Women" by *Good Housekeeping* magazine

Becomes ill again and spends time recovering in Colorado

1931–32

Proposed as executive officer of the Federal Emergency Relief Board in the first Congressional bills attempting to combat the Great Depression

1933–39

Serves as adviser to U.S. Secretary of Labor Frances Perkins

1934

Resigns as chief of the Children's Bureau

Returns to the University of Chicago to teach as a professor of public welfare and to serve as managing editor of the *Social Service Review*

1934–35

Works on preparation and passage of the Social Security Act by drafting welfare programs regarding aid to dependent children, services for disabled children, and maternal and infant health

Serves as a member of President Franklin Roosevelt's Council on Economic Security

1935

Goes to Geneva to serve as chairperson of the U.S. delegation to the International Labor Organization Conference

Serves as chair of the Committee on Unemployment of Young Persons and urges that the minimum age for leaving school and starting work be raised to fifteen

Asked to succeed Jane Addams as head of Hull House but declines for health reasons

Offered a post as one of three Social Security Board members but declines for health reasons

June

Othman Ali Abbott dies

1936

Grace attends the National Conference of Social Work in Atlantic City

1937

Testifies before the Interstate Commerce Committee in Washington DC

Works for the "Children's Amendment" to the U.S. Constitution

Chairs the U.S. Delegation to the Pan American Conference (International Labor Organization Conference) in Mexico City where she is a reporter for the Committee on Minimum Age and is responsible for the resolution regarding the protection of the legal, social, and industrial position of women

Appeals to the Nebraska legislature for the "Children's Amendment," which Nebraska fails to ratify

Elizabeth Abbott is awarded an honorary degree by Rockford College; Grace receives it on her behalf

1938

Serves on the Textile Committee under the new "Wages and Hours Administration"

Grace's work toward the federal prohibition of child labor is partially realized in the Fair Labor Standards Act

Diagnosed with multiple myeloma

Writes *The Child and the State*

1939 *March*

Grace's health continues to fail, and she breaks her arm

1939 *June 19*

Grace dies in Chicago and is buried in Grand Island, Nebraska

The Grace Abbott Reader

PART I

Immigrants

Perhaps no one in America did more to put an end to the exploitation of immigrants than did Grace Abbott.

—WILLIAM L. CHENERY, Editor, *Collier's Weekly*

Hull House Days

Edith Abbott
From "A Sister's Memories," ca. 1952[1]

"Jane Addams" and "Hull House" were almost magic words to people
back in the spring of 1908 when my sister Grace—by now a young
political science student at the University of Chicago—was unex-
pectedly offered the opportunity of a great adventure: moving to
Halsted Street with Miss Addams and working on an experimental
new project for the immigrants of Chicago.

Hull House was quite famous. But why? It was the first American
social settlement, that's true, but I must admit that—back then just as
today—there was not really much interest in social work among the
public. No, Hull House was known because Miss Addams had made
it a beautiful place for people who lived in an area of the city where
nothing else was beautiful, and because she had brought together a
group of men and women to live and work with her—not as charity
workers, but as friends—in one of the tenement neighborhoods
of the great city. Hull House was known because it was something
wonderfully strange.

The new project that Miss Addams planned in 1908 was an organization to be known as the Immigrants' Protective League,[2] and
she first approached Sophonisba Breckinridge, our friend at the
University of Chicago, about taking charge of the organization. When
Miss Breckinridge refused to leave the University to direct the new
League herself, Miss Addams had asked her if she couldn't "find a
competent man" to be her assistant while she gave part of her time

to the new organization. Miss Breckinridge said very quickly, "We don't need to waste any time looking for a man. We have a young woman, Grace Abbott, in the political science department who will be much better than any man that I know or can possibly find." As a result, Grace was urged to take the position as director of the new Immigrants' League to see what could be done. She gave up her graduate work and went to the West Side to begin a long period of residence at Hull House, which was then the center of one of Chicago's great immigrant receiving areas.

Soon I joined her there, for I had recently made plans to give up my job of teaching economics in a woman's college back East, gladly accepting the invitation of Miss Breckinridge to join her in developing a new school for teaching social work, which was also to be given space in one of the Hull House buildings.

I was so glad to come back to Chicago that I forgot about the steaming summer heat and the smells in the Hull House neighborhood. They seemed only part of the welcome contrast between the vigorous activity of Chicago's Halsted Street and the cool aloofness of a New England college for women. When I returned to Chicago in June, 1908, I found Grace already settled at Hull House as if she were among old friends.

Hull House was still a part of a vast city wilderness when first we went there to live . . . the conditions more primitive than those of the prairie frontier Grace had only recently left behind. Rotting stables were everywhere and the alleys were indescribably filthy. The tenements were—many of them—no more than wooden shacks that had been built on the prairie before the Great Fire: tiny sordid rooms with no windows, no electricity, no water, crammed with the bodies of sometimes a dozen boarders. They were beyond description. But there was an eclectic kind of beauty to the area, as well.

The Hull House life was always full of new interests. There was something unique about the group of residents, a mixture of professional men and women, some of them able and experienced, and others just beginning to learn something of neighborhood work.

Usually there were from twenty to twenty-five women residents—twelve of us living with Miss Addams in the old part of the house that had once been the home of the Hull family, and the others living in apartments which were built around what we called "the court," a nice stretch of grass with a few small trees and shrubs and some walks that led to the different buildings. Then there were a dozen men in the two upper floors of the men's residence, one of the buildings attached to the old house, and there were always other men and women and a few children in the apartments.

Best of all was a residents' dining room where we had dinner together and a residents' breakfast table in the public coffee shop where we argued, in relays, over the morning newspapers. Although we were a large number of residents, we were a kind of family group together—a very argumentative family group. Our political opinions varied widely, and our arguments not infrequently began at the breakfast table. During the day, the various participants in the current controversy seemed to have sharpened their weapons and prepared for the new arguments that were sure to be heard at the dinner table, with Miss Addams often serving as mediator and laughing as verbal shots were fired. In the late evening hours, the arguments were still going on with those who sat around together when the House was officially closed and the neighbors had all gone home and the residents could use the reception room and the library for themselves.

Our life there was more interesting precisely because we belonged to different political groups and worked in different organizations. Grace often said that we learned in the Hull House days to have both affection and respect for those who didn't agree with us.

Among the residents in those days were two Russians who had come from the oppression of the czar in the days when they had both been revolutionists. During the first World War, a woman who had escaped from Siberia joined them, and after the Russian Revolution, there came others. After one of our long arguments at the Hull House dinner table, the woman from Siberia laughed and said, "I haven't felt so much at home since I first joined the Terrorists!"

But for all this joy, there were hard times, too, especially when some family in the neighborhood were having difficulties and we looked after their appeals. One family was regularly in trouble because of the man's drinking. He was sometimes violent when he was drunk, and harsh and even cruel to the children. The woman would come to us frightened and say, "He's wild again, and I don't know what to do." Grace and I went home with her one night to see whether we ought to call the police. The woman was clearly anxious and kept telling us how violent "he" had been.

When we arrived, the children were frightened and crying. "Mr. Egan," said Grace firmly and sternly to the man, "go to bed."

He shuffled off and the woman, seeing his docility to Grace said, "I think we'll be all right now, Miss Abbott. Thank you." Sometimes she would telephone us late at night and say, "I feel better after I've heard your voice, Miss Abbott. I don't feel so alone."

Finally, we took the desperate step of telling the woman that she should have the man sent to the House of Correction for nonsupport. Should we have advised her as we did, we asked ourselves? Grace and I always thought that just sending a man to jail was a confession of incompetence. In this case, we had helped send him to jail because we simply didn't know what else to do. "A poor excuse for us," was Grace's comment.

ONE

The Immigrant Girl

From "Within the City's Gates," *Chicago Evening Post,*
December 23, 1909[1]

Any woman can understand the nervous apprehension which the immigrant girl must feel as she comes into one of Chicago's bewildering railroad stations, but very few realize how well grounded her fears are. Friends and relatives find it impossible to meet them because immigrant trains are sidetracked for all other kinds of traffic, so that no one can determine when they are to arrive.

Not long ago I met an immigrant train that came in at the Polk Street station, and I understood better the stories the girls tell us. This train was due at seven-thirty in the morning, but arrived shortly after four in the afternoon, and I had to make three trips to the station, although I telephoned each time before starting.

Several hundred girls got off the train. Many of them were very young, and I felt their disappointment as they peered eagerly and anxiously about for the father or sister or friend they expected to see. Those who were going North or West came out the main gate, already ticketed by a representative of the transfer company, and were transferred without any confusion just as other travelers are.

But those who were to remain in Chicago were directed into a small immigrant waiting room which opens on Federal Street. Here they were hastily sorted into groups and then pushed out the door into the midst of ten or twelve expressmen who were crowding and pushing and quarreling over the division of spoils. In a short time the struggle was over and they had all been loaded into the waiting wagons.

By this time it was almost dark and I watched them drive away with many misgivings. For I remembered the little Irish girl who told us she started on a wagon with a group of other immigrants for the South Side. After going some distance, the expressman discovered she had a North Side address, so charging her four dollars, he put her off the wagon without any suggestion as to what she should do.

And then, too, I remembered the Polish girl of seventeen who was taken at three o'clock in the morning to the place where her sister was supposed to live. But the address was incorrect and the woman who lived there angrily refused to let her stay until morning. She had only a few dollars and wept disconsolately when the expressman told her "nobody could find her sister if nobody knew her address, and that he wasn't going to take her back for nothing." The saloonkeeper next door finally offered her a refuge and she lived with his family behind the saloon three days before her sister, who was making daily trips to the depot, was found.

§

Officials and officers at the Grand Central Station feel a certain responsibility for the women and children who come in at the station, and require the expressmen to bring back to the depot all those whose friends or relatives are not found. From there they are usually referred to the League. Not long ago a twelve-year-old German boy was brought to the office in this way. The policeman assured him that we would take good care of him, but he found it very hard to be brave when he faced the fact that he was hungry and without money, and that his big brother who had sent him his ticket and was going to look out for him, could not be found. While the boy was being cared for, a visitor for the League started on the trail of the brother. He was found before night, although he had moved three times since he left the place the address of which his little brother had brought. The steamship agent had promised to notify him when the boy would arrive, and he had carefully kept the agent informed about the change of his address.

§

If the United States immigration department would establish a protective bureau ... the situation might be greatly improved. ... There should be one central place in Chicago to which those who are expecting friends or relatives from Europe might go and learn whether they had come, and to whom they had been released.

Only this morning the distracted relatives of a young Polish woman, who telegraphed that she was leaving Ellis Island Nov. 16 and has not been heard from since, were in the office asking us to find the girl. We may be able to trace her, but the only official information will be the record of when she left Ellis Island. No one knows who are expected and never arrive.

TWO

The Education of Foreigners in American Citizenship

From the Report of the School Extension Committee, 1910

The importance of the task of preparing for American citizenship our yearly additions of foreigners is little appreciated by the American public. In Chicago we have something like thirty-six nationalities represented in our population, and Chicago's population is not more complex than that of most American cities. More than two-thirds of its people are either "foreign born" or "native born of foreign parentage," and the remaining one-third is attempting to make the necessary adjustments among these thirty-six groups and at the same time to bring them all under a dominating American influence. If one were to ask the average American how these people are initiated into our social, industrial, and political life, he would probably tell you either that it was not accomplished at all, and that we ought to keep out "these hordes of Europeans"; or else he would say that he knew nothing of the process, but it was being done. He was sure it was, because look at this, that or the other great and distinguished American who had come to the country fifteen or twenty years ago with no assets except his own courage and thrift, and was now a great power for good in the community. As a matter of fact, both these points of view are in a certain sense right. We are absorbing the immigrant into our national life, but the question is, are we doing it intelligently and economically or with a recklessly extravagant disregard for the men and women who are lost in the process.

As a community we are relying upon the public schools to accomplish this work of Americanization, in the belief that if the children are properly trained, the future will take care of itself, for the parents are only a one-generation difficulty anyway. While this disregard of the possible usefulness or danger in the thousands of men and women who come to us every year results in great loss to the community, the assumption which seems to justify it is unwarranted, for the immigrant child cannot be properly trained in American citizenship if nothing is done for his parents.

Apparently our settled policy in the treatment of our foreign population is to ignore the fact that they are foreign. As though—by pretending that the Italian's social, industrial and political traditions are the same as ours—they will, by some miracle, become so. This has been the great American faith-cure treatment for the difficulties which come from our complex population, the results of which have not always justified the faith.

In the case of the children, we have probably incorrectly assumed that the training which the immigrant child needs is the same as the training which the American born child should have. Under the present system American habits of dress, speech, and manners are very rapidly acquired, and in the narrow field of teaching reading, writing and arithmetic the schools have probably met the expectations of the public. But this equipment is not proving an adequate protection for the immigrant child against the temptations which he has to meet. Although the percentage of crime is smaller among our foreign-born citizens than among the native-born Americans, the records of the juvenile court show that more than three-fourths of the children brought into the court are of foreign parentage. These children have not, of course, committed "crimes" in most cases. Any man whose boyhood included the larks usual to that age would be apt to conclude, after reading over the Illinois or Colorado definition of delinquency, that it was just as well there were no juvenile courts when he was a boy, for he would have been the despair of judge and probation officer. But this would not, of course, have been the case. The American father or mother whose child commits these small violations of the law, understanding the situation, is able by the substitution of a new and wholesome interest for the dangerous one to prevent the commission of more serious offenses. But the immigrant parent finds this extremely difficult to do. His children, because of the rapid strides they have made in the public schools, have become the interpreters of America to him. Many things which the old-world father or mother frowns on, "all the kids do here"—a statement sometimes correct and at other times dangerously incorrect. The American mother who has found herself quite helpless before a similar argument which clearly indicated that the girl or boy thought her standards old-fashioned, can appreciate in some measure the difficulty of the Italian or Polish parents. For them it is much intensified by their peculiar dependence upon their children. They speak to the boss, the landlord, the policeman—all the great in their world—through their children. In such a family the oldest child usually refers to the children as "mine." "My fader's gotter get work because my Charlie haint got no shoes," he explains as the reason for making an appeal to you for advice as to where his father's services may find a market. And when this boy or girl after going to work is able, because of his knowledge of English and familiarity with certain American customs, to earn more than the father, family relationships are completely reversed. When such a child becomes tired of the burden of responsibility which he has so early assumed and makes a few gay excursions with his gang, his father's word of warning is little heeded and so the assistants of the judge of the juvenile court and the probation officers are trying to do this, but with the best intentions in the world we are usually widening the gap between the parent and the child by the policy we are following in our public schools. In our zeal to teach patriotism, we are often teaching disrespect for the history and traditions which the immigrant parent had a part in making, and so for the parent himself. Some teachers, with a quick appreciation of the difficulty the family is meeting in the sudden change of national heroes and standards, are able to avoid mistakes of this sort by making it clear that the story of the struggle for Italian nationalism is a thrilling one to us, and that Bohemian leaders, because of their long fight for religious liberty, are heroes to Americans. A little Greek boy who is a friend of mine explained, "My teacher likes me because I tell her stories of the Athens." Whether Miss O'Grady really cared for the stories he told of the city from which so few of our Greek immigrants come and yet whose history and traditions are so intimately loved by them, I cannot say. But I do know that both the school and Athens occupied a different place in the eyes of the boy because of the seeming interest of the teacher. Such results should not be left to the casual interests of the teacher. In every foreign neighborhood the transition from the old to the new world heroes and ideals should be very carefully worked out or else the change will result disastrously for either the parent or the child.

Respect for the father's work ought also to be taught. In one part of Chicago, which is known as Grand Crossing, the life of the neighborhood centers in the elevation of the network of railroad tracks which cross there in entering the city. A very intelligent superintendent of this district made this undertaking the basis of a large part of the regular school work. The children made models in wood and clay and paper of the completed work and of the machinery and tools which were used. Little essays explained the need of the work and who was responsible for its being undertaken. All of this was in accordance with the soundest pedagogical principles since "all school training must adapt itself to the background of life which the children live," but equally important, it was giving to the children a new respect for the work their fathers did, and I have no doubt that in the minds of the men themselves, what had been merely a means of livelihood became, in a way, a public service.

. . . But however well the children may be taught, however ingeniously we may try to reach the parent through the child, we will fail in our ultimate purpose of making the best possible citizens of the children, unless the community concerns itself actively in the education of the adult immigrant.

The great majority of people who come to us from Europe are young people between fifteen and thirty years of age. All of them know something of the industrial conditions in America—that is a reason for their coming. But of labor laws designed for their protection, of the employment agent and his practices, of possible markets for their skill, of what is a fair wage in America, they know nothing at all. All of them know we have a republican form of government. That, too, is a reason for their coming. Most of them know something also of the history of the country and of the principles which it has championed before the world. But of the American political machinery by which we attempt to put into practice our republican principles, they know nothing. In most cities, all that we are offering this army of young men and women is instruction in English in our night schools. Even this is often so poorly done as to discourage all but the most ambitious or the hopelessly stupid. One still finds large classes of men crowded into seats intended for children of ten or fifteen years of age, reading from a primer of the "see the cat on the mat" variety. Some books whose words and pictures are based on the work and life of the men have been published recently and are making possible much better instruction than formerly. Miss Addams tells the story of one eager teacher who, feeling the need of some connection between the life of the class and the teaching of English, prepared a series of lessons.[1] The class was to begin with the sentence "I get up early every morning." That in theory was to be followed by "I wash my face," and so on until they had been through the regular morning routine as she conceived it. The plan was explained to the class, a group of Italian girls, who could speak some English but could not read or write. They were all home finishers of men's ready-made clothes—at that time one of the sweated industries in Chicago. The girls entered enthusiastically on the plan. They began according to the scheme with "I get up early every morning," but followed in concert with "I sew pants all day." With these girls, as with the rest of us, the work they were doing seemed the important thing, and eating and washing were after all mere details, relegated to the background when it came to a discussion of the day's program. It is needless to say that after that the lessons given the girls were based on the tailoring trade.

. . . But many Americans are not satisfied with the teaching of English alone. They want instructions in what they call the fundamental American principles. When I have tried to discover just what they have in mind, I have usually found they feel it would be a good thing to put immediately into the immigrant's hands the story of Lincoln and Washington, and that patriotic instruction should be made the basis of all of their future work. Of course none of us can read too often the story of these men or others who have stood for great causes in the history of the world, but the most sincere admirer of Lincoln would not contend that his utterances would serve as a practical guide in the election of aldermen. The fundamental Americanisms, I am convinced, cannot be taught by the method of direct assault, so to speak, and we should not be discouraged at failures when it is used. Probably we would put the principle of religious toleration well along toward the first of the characteristics which we regard as distinctly American, and are especially anxious to cherish. But when I think how long it took to Americanize my own Puritan ancestors, judged by this test, I hope no one will be discouraged if the Italian fails to learn it in a course of ten lessons in the fundamentals.

Many Americans, as a matter of fact, regard as of first importance a change in the superficial habits—the speech, dress, and house-keeping—of the immigrants. And yet no one of us really sees any danger in the use of black bread instead of white, or in wearing a shawl instead of a hat. Americanization in these things will come rapidly enough. What we must do, if the immigrant is to become a desirable citizen, is to preserve his simple honesty and thrift, and his faith in America and American institutions. As the first step in this process, he needs to know almost immediately on his arrival the practices of employment agents and the remedies that are open to him in cases of abuse; the requirements for licenses in certain trades;

something of our labor laws; something of our sanitary regulations; how he may protect himself against violations by his neighbors of the health code; and how he may send home money to his wife or his mother. These are the things which the public schools should be giving the immigrant in his own language by means of illustrated lectures. To wait until the immigrant learns these things in the school of bitter experience is not only to make him suffer an unnecessary financial loss, but his future usefulness is much impaired if he is exploited and robbed from the moment of his arrival. Consequently, it is important from the standpoint of the community's good that he be given this initial instruction. Following this, there should be a course in the practical workings of the American government, also in the language of the immigrant. With the sort of instruction in English usually given the immigrant—and even with the very best instruction—he is unable to understand any difficult presentation of facts in English, although he may have been here for some years. And he is, therefore, quite dependent upon his native language in any preparation for naturalization and the responsibility of citizenship. Instruction can be given by means of a "guide" which contains all there is to be known about America, but he finds reading difficult and can be reached only by practical instruction in our public schools. There need be no fear that the use of another language in any way menaces the continued use of the English language in America. There is no danger that the Bohemian children in the Bohemian neighborhood are not going to learn to talk English. But there is a very real danger that those children are not going to become the sort of men and women we want them to, unless we do something for their Bohemian parents. The public libraries are undertaking to meet the cultural demands of these groups of foreigners by supplying them with books in their own language. The public schools should become a real educational center for the adults as well as the children of the neighborhood. Then a very different sort of preparation for citizenship would be possible.

After they have been trained in this way, the tests for naturalization could be made quite different.[2] . . . Respect for naturalization would be much increased if some sort of impressive ceremony were used. This is the only way in which Old World people, who are accustomed to dignified procedure, can be made to feel that they are entering upon a new period in their life. I know several young people now who have been planning and talking to me for a year and a half about their coming naturalization this winter. I feel somewhat embarrassed to find them anticipate it as a great event, for I know it will be treated as a trivial matter in the court, and there will be no recognition on the part of the community of the great change in their relation to the nation. I understand that in Rochester, the citizens give a dinner to the newly-naturalized citizens, and that there are addresses and responses, and a sort of welcome into the community of citizens. Something of this sort is greatly needed in every city.

. . . In these days when we are learning through our study of public expenditure the cost to the city of the things we are leaving undone as well as those we are doing, we may hope that some one will be able to estimate the cost to the community of spending neither time, thought, nor money on the question of making Americans out of the million people who are coming to us every year.

THREE

The Immigrant as a Problem
in Community Planning

From *Publications of the American Sociological Society,*
vol. 21, 1917

In the discussion of immigration during the past century attention
has been concentrated almost wholly on what immigrants we should
exclude from the United States and little attention has been given
to the admitted immigrant. Since the beginning of the Great War
a new interest in the foreign born who is here in our midst has
developed. With the stimulation of nationalism there has come a
new consciousness of the diverse elements in our population. As a
result the indifference of some native Americans has been changed
to distrust and suspicion of all the foreign born; many have come to
feel that what they call the "alien element" constitutes a very heavy
national burden. Some are asking whether anything that is really
thoroughgoing has been done to Americanize the immigrant in the
past; they are now saying that we ought to "mold" the newcomers after
some approved American pattern, and are eager to get them into
a room and tell them about "American ideals." Curiously enough,
these enthusiastic Americanizers see no reflection on ourselves in
the assumption that the immigrant could live among us for several
years and never guess what our ideals are from our practices.

. . . The duty and the opportunity of the national government
and of the local community to the admitted immigrant were and
still are (1) to protect him against fraud and exploitation, so that
such traditions as he cherished with regard to America might not
be lost in his first contacts with us; (2) to give him an opportunity to

learn the English language and secure such working knowledge of our laws and institutions as would enable him to join us in the work of making the U.S. a really effective democracy; (3) to make such adjustments of our political and social machinery as the peculiar needs of the various elements in our complex population render necessary or desirable.

. . . We have been satisfied to leave to the evening-school teacher, who has had no training in the teaching of adults, who is poorly paid and who, like those whom she instructs, comes to the night school wearied by a full day's work—to this teacher and to the party-machine organization we have entrusted the preparation of the immigrant for American citizenship. There is no necessity to continue to point out what the immigrant has suffered needlessly because of community neglect.

Let us assume that a community asks how it may prevent unnecessary failures among its foreign-born and how it may utilize to the fullest the potential contribution of each national group. Such a community would have to determine, as its first step, whether the present institutions were established and administered with a view to serving only a homogenous Anglo-Saxon population, or whether the needs of the real, instead of the imaginary, population had been considered. To determine this, it is necessary to know the political, social, and economic life of the peasants in their European homes, as well as the special difficulties which they are encountering here in the United States.[1]

Everyone knows that the immigrants coming to the United States usually change from a simple to a highly specialized and complex industrial life when they come from Galicia, or Croatia, or Russia to America.[2] During their first years in this country they must, in consequence, abandon many old customs and adopt new standards of social relationship. They are usually young and suddenly released from the restraints which the village life at home imposed upon them and they have had no experience on which to draw during the critical period when they are becoming adjusted to the new conditions. Most of them meet this crisis simply and, in a measure, successfully. Sometimes, however, a tragic moral collapse or a general demoralization of family standards results from the inability of the immigrant to adjust his old standards to the new. Before any progress can be made toward eliminating the hardships of adjustment to American life these difficulties must be recognized and understood. The school teacher, the social worker, the judge of the juvenile or the municipal court, is unable to help the immigrant out of his confused bewilderment unless he understands, not in a general way but quite concretely, the conflict with traditional standards of judgment which his life in the new world has brought.

To many Americans the so-called foreign colonies in New York, Chicago, Pittsburgh, or Cleveland seem to be reproductions of sections of Italy, Greece, Poland, or Russia. But to the immigrant the street on which he lives here is so unlike the one on which he lived at home that he believes it to be thoroughly American. These "foreign neighborhoods" of ours are neither Italian, nor Polish, nor Russian, nor Greek. Nor are they American. A sympathetic knowledge of the life and hopes of the people of these un-American American neighborhoods is rare among us. An understanding of the racial history, of the social and economic development, and of present political tendencies in the countries from which the inhabitants of such a neighborhood come is much more unusual. A knowledge of both their life here and their life at home is necessary for intelligent community planning. In the attempts made to help those who have been unable to make the necessary adjustments to the new conditions they encounter here, we have usually acted quite without the information which is necessary for the proper diagnosis of the source of their difficulties, and as long as individual cases are not properly diagnosed successful treatment is only a happy accident and cannot form the basis for a program of prevention.

In general, the immigrant does not create new problems that can be solved apart from the general problems of our community life. This is not saying that he does not complicate American life.

The barriers of language, the inherited antipathies and religious prejudices, cannot be ignored as sources of difficulties. These constitute serious complications which must be taken into account in our social planning.

To illustrate, our failure to effect an organization of the employment market has resulted in unnecessary hardships for all those who seek employment. The development of a system of labor exchanges is recommended as a remedy. But a system of public employment agencies would not serve the immigrant who is so peculiarly in need of disinterested help when he offers himself in the labor market, if such an agency has no interpreters, and if those who undertake to advise the immigrant about his industrial future cannot evaluate his European training or experience or the lack of both, and if they do not understand the peculiar industrial problems which the non-English-speaking immigrant encounters here. A recreation program which is designed to reduce delinquency among girls will not meet the needs of the immigrant girl until special forms of recreation have been discovered which will appeal to the young people of each nationality, and which will not run counter to the social traditions of their parents. A public-health program will not reach the immigrant when he most needs it, unless it is related to his old-world experience and given to him in a language he can understand. Because he is changing from an outdoor to an indoor life, from a village to a city, he especially needs to be reached by the public-health propaganda long before he has had time to learn the English language and become acquainted with local conditions.

It is apparent to a growing number of people in the United States and Europe that fundamental changes in our social and political organization must be made in the near future. The causes which make this necessary and the evils to be corrected, while differing in degree, are the same on both continents. With us, because the immigrant is the weakest industrially he suffers most from the evils of the present system. His peculiar problems and difficulties must therefore be considered in any plans for the democratization of industry.

The problem of the immigrant in relation to our community life is then not so much a problem in assimilation as in adjustment. To assist in such adjustments, we must take account, first, of those traditions and characteristics which belong to the immigrants by reason of their race and early environment and, second, of the peculiar difficulties which they encounter here. These two elements in the problem must be known before we can hope to reach conclusions.

It need not be pointed out that it is impossible to work out any permanent scheme of adjustment. Changes in the sources of immigration must be constantly kept in mind. Advancing social and educational standards will make for both the immigrant and the native American what is adequate today, inadequate tomorrow. But what we are trying to do will remain the same. We should ask ourselves what special provision must be made to protect those among us whose helplessness makes their need of protection so great; what should be done to supplement the immigrant's as well as the native American's lack of training and experience; how, in other words, to make the best that is in all of us, available for the service of the whole community.

There are Americans who resent the immigrant as an outsider, whose troubles they should not be asked to consider. Some feel that to take account deliberately in our social planning of differences in customs and traditions would be a dangerous recognition of un-Americanisms. But as a rule, neither of these reasons has determined our course. It is usually because of ignorance and indifference that in our social policies we have failed to consider the complex character of our population, and have built our social and political institutions with a view to meeting the needs of an imaginary homogenous people.

Those Americans who resent the immigrant as an outsider and are, in consequence, impatient of any demands which his presence makes upon their time or thought or money are the same people who stand in the way of meeting in a large sense the needs of the native born. They consider our institutions more important than the ends those institutions were created to serve. We may feel sure that if our administrative officers understand the necessity of individualizing the needs of the American born they will be willing to individualize the needs of the immigrant groups.

An intelligent recognition of the complications and possible disadvantages of our cosmopolitan population does not mean that we should ignore its advantages. How many of what are called American traits are due to geographical influence, to frontier life, or to diverse racial contributions cannot be determined by conjecture. To what extent the Scandinavians have made the history of Minnesota different from the history of North Carolina or Colorado or Massachusetts cannot be exactly determined. It is even more difficult to say what influence the Scandinavians might have exerted were they not controlled or limited by the common insistence on what is regarded an American standard. But that into the development of Minnesota have gone Scandinavian intelligence, hard work, and devotion to the larger public welfare cannot be questioned.

It has always been embarrassing to Americans to have distinguished visitors from abroad call attention to the fact that the United States is not a "nation" in the European sense of the word. It is true that unity of religion, unity of race, unity of ideals do not exist in the United States. Whether such unity should be sought in a democracy need not be considered here. From the beginning we have been the representatives of many nationalities; now we are scattered across a continent with all the additional differences in interest and occupation that diversity of climate and geography brings. But instead of being ashamed of the "American" character of our population, it is time that we recognized its peculiar values.

The demand for a recognition of "nationalism" in Europe is the democratic demand that all the peoples should be free to associate together as equals. They have argued that equality is impossible if a people is not free to speak the language which they prefer and to develop their own national culture and character. Here in the United States we have the opportunity of working out a national life which is founded on democratic internationalism. If the English, Irish, Polish, German, Scandinavian, Russian, Magyar, Lithuanian and all other peoples of the earth can live together, each making his own distinctive contribution to our common life; if we can respect the differences that result from the different social and political environment and see the common interests that unite all people, we shall meet the American opportunity. This will mean that we shall endeavor to use both at home and in our international relationship the possibilities which are ours because we are of many races and are related, by the closest of human ties, to all the world.

Out of the very fact that here in the United States all the races of the world are working together in a single city, in a single industry, or are united in a single union local should come a new kind of power. As never before we are realizing the international aspects of what have seemed to be merely national or local problems. It remains to be seen whether we will use our national international resources in their solution.

"Americanism" is much more a matter of the future than of the past. The social and political theories of '76 cannot adequately meet the social and political problems of 1917. It is to be hoped that we can bring to the problems of the present an intelligence and understanding which will enable us to meet these opportunities and responsibilities of the present.

FOUR

Problems of the Immigrant Girl

From *The Immigrant and the Community*, 1917

As one thinks of this great stream of Polish, Russian, Jewish, Italian, Ruthenian, Lithuanian, and all the other girls who have been coming from the country districts of southern and eastern Europe, one wonders how they had the courage to undertake this excursion into the unknown. Several years ago, while studying the districts in Galicia, in northern Hungary, and in Croatia, from which so many girls have come to the United States, I kept asking myself and those whom I met this one question. A professor in the Polish University of Lemberg . . . told me that the first thing I needed to understand in any study of emigration from this region was that the peasants did not go because they needed work; there was plenty of work for them there; he knew landlords whose crops were rotting in the ground because the men and women of the neighborhood had all gone to America. It was a fever that was running through the entire peasantry, he explained. They went to the United States as he might go to the next street.

A few days later, I visited the region he had described to me. It was in the autumn, when the principal food of the peasantry—potatoes and cabbages—was being stored away for use during the long winter. On the largest estate of the neighborhood I looked in amazement at a potato field on which there were so many people working that they almost touched elbows as they moved across the field. Guided by the priest, I visited all the types of houses in the village—the poorest as well as the best. At first, one felt the appeal of the picturesque, for the fields were gay with the bright peasant costumes of the girls, and the low, thatched-roof cottages had been freshly whitewashed and had flowers in the queer little windows.

But there was nothing picturesque about the dirt floors, the absence of chimneys and furniture, and the long distance that all the water had to be carried. When it was dark, most of the population gathered in the village square, where the girls were paid about twenty-five cents for their day's work. I followed them into the little church for the vesper service; and, as I looked at the patient, tired faces of these girls, I understood why it was that they could not start for America until letters had come bringing them tickets from the Galician village to the city in the U.S. where a brother or sister or a friend is already established. I understood, too, why, when the tickets came, they would start, without hesitating at the dangers they might meet on the journey or the possibility that failure might await them at the other end.

A little to the west of this village there was another where economic conditions were much better. There was a sugar factory, a distillery, a big dairy; and the great landlord of the neighborhood had a beautifully kept estate and farms, which employed many peasants.

The houses, too, were better. There were wooden floors, chimneys, more tiled and fewer thatched roofs; and there were fruit trees round each house. Instead of the small, dirty, and poorly furnished elementary school of the first village, there were a kindergarten and a gymnasium in addition to an elementary school. In this neighborhood there were organizations of peasant men and women for the promotion of more scientific farming. In a domestic science class there were about thirty girls of high school age learning sewing, cooking, laundry work, and something of the farm industries. When they were asked how many of them had girl friends in America, the hands went up all round the room, and then in response to the question how many were coming themselves, and again how many were coming to Chicago, there were still many hands. It was not economic necessity that was sending them. I came, however, to understand why they, too, desired to try life in America.

Forced labor was abolished in Austria in 1848; but it was not until 1867 and 1869 that the right of the peasant to divide his land was made general, so that serfdom remained, in a sense, until that time. As I talked with the landlords of the neighborhood, I found that, like the Southern white man in his attitude toward the Negro, they were indulgently tolerant of the faults of the peasantry, but were convinced that these faults were due to the fact that the peasants were a quite different order of human beings from themselves. They laughed at us for taking the peasants so seriously and imagining we could make ladies and gentlemen of them. The peasants, they were sure, were all "spoiled" by an American experience. The older peasants are themselves sometimes equally conservative in their devotion to the old social order; so the ambitious young peasant has the opposition of his own class as well as the class prejudice of those above him to overcome.

Whether or not it is completely reasoned out by the peasant who undertakes the journey, this class feeling is an important cause of emigration. It is much simpler to break entirely with the past, to abandon the picturesque costume, the little farm, the dependence on the landlord of the neighborhood, and to stake everything on a possible success in America than to try to break down the century-old social barriers of the village. In other words, it was the fact that apparently nothing could change either for themselves or for their children, which sent many of these women from Austria and Hungary to America.

§

. . . The immigrant girls do not realize their handicaps, and usually begin work in the United States without any of the doubts and anxious fears which many of us have for them. Being young, they believe that the world must hold something good in store for them. In the faith that America feels kindly toward them they expect to find here among us that happy future to which all girls look forward. And in this expectation these young foreign women and girls undertake the great American adventure.

Those of us who can remember our own great expectations as we left college and the anxious fears of that first year of our "independence" can, perhaps, understand the greater crisis which the immigrant girl faces in her first year in the United States.

Most of them are, at first, homesick and disappointed. The streets of the city are not always broad and beautiful, and life not always gay and bright as they had hoped it would be. On the contrary, the experience of the Russian-Jewish girl who came to a cousin on Liberty Street in Chicago is not unusual. A returned immigrant translated to her the word "Liberty," and she imagined that she was coming to live on an avenue which would symbolize all that one bearing that precious name should. But she found her cousin living in a rear house on a short, narrow, unpaved, dirty street. The houses on Liberty Street are as poor as any Chicago knows, and there is no place where poverty seems more intimate and its ugliness more inevitable. After a short experience in a tailor shop, she had to give up the struggle. She did not live long enough to know anything about the United States except the disappointment of Liberty Street.

Sometimes it seems to the peasant girls as if they had exchanged the green fields and woods and the long, quiet winters for a hideous round of noise, heat, and bitter cold.

. . . How many of them give way under the strain of long hours, bad living conditions, and the confused excitement which comes with their new environment, few people realize. The tragedy of this physical breakdown was illustrated one summer when the services of the Immigrants' Protective League were asked on behalf of a young Polish girl. Although she seemed entirely well when she came and had been passed by the examining doctors at Ellis Island, she had developed tuberculosis after a few months of factory work in Chicago. She was taken to the County Hospital and soon learned that she had no chance of recovery. She was most wretchedly homesick when the visitor for the League saw her at the hospital. She had only a cousin in this country, who could not come to see her because it was the season of overtime work in his trade and the County Hospital was many miles away. She was unable to talk to those around her and found it impossible to eat the strange American food given her, and, worst of all, she realized that all of her girlish plans to earn money, send for her mother, and marry well were to come to nothing. Polish food which we were able to procure for her did not comfort her, however, for she wanted only one thing—to be sent back home so that she might die with her mother. In this, too, she was disappointed, for although she improved somewhat when she learned that she was to be deported, she died alone at sea.

§

There are many explanations for the fact that the immigrant girls sometimes become unmarried mothers. There is the greater helplessness which is due to their ignorance of English; there is also the more dangerous environment in which they live, for it is near an immigrant or colored neighborhood that disreputable dance halls and hotels are usually tolerated. Moreover, their recreational needs are less understood than those of the native-born American, and the break with the old-world traditions has left them with fewer standards of discrimination.

At home, the girls have been accustomed to out-of-door dances and sports. In Chicago, when Saturday night comes, the demand for some sort of excitement after a hard and uneventful week, has become too strong to be ignored. But the danger is that because of her physical and nervous exhaustion and her demand for acute sense stimulation, the girl will become an easy victim for the unscrupulous. The neighboring saloon keeper, alert to the business side of her needs, is constantly seeking to attract her to the dance hall which he conducts in the rear of his saloon. At its best, such a dance adds to the nervous demoralization which began with the girl's overfatigue. At its worst, it leaves her disgraced and ruined. An extension of Chicago's admirable system of parks and playgrounds or a wider use of the public schools while helpful, is not enough to meet this situation. For these girls must first be given sufficient leisure to enable them to enjoy the wholesome recreation and opportunities for self-advancement which the city is offering them. This, they are not able to do after ten hours of scrubbing or coremaking six days in a week.

§

The immigrant girl has a long and hard road to travel. She suffers from the industrial and legal discriminations which are the common lot of working women. In addition, she must overcome the stupid race prejudice which leads many Americans to conclude that she suffers less from shame and humiliation than do other women and girls. Without trade training and with little education, as a rule, she begins at the bottom industrially, where, if the wages of the men are low, the wages of the girls are still lower.

And yet, in this struggle in which they are so handicapped, these girls are winning little by little—often at a terrible cost to their health and, in consequence, to the health of the children they will bear in the future. There are many who are moved only by this danger to the future generations. But for the girls of this generation, we should ask more leisure, better pay, better homes, and more sympathy before they are too old and broken to enjoy the fruits of their toil and of their eager sacrifices.

PART II

Children

My dear Miss Abbott, you have rendered service of inestima-
ble value to the children and mothers and fathers of the country, as well as to federal and state governments.

In expressing my appreciation of the constructive policies
of permanent value which you inaugurated and your exceptional ability as a far-sighted administrator, I am also voicing
that of the boys and girls and men and women all over the
country who have reaped their rich benefits.

I am sure that you will continue to contribute greatly to the
well-being of the children of the nation. May you have every
success. I have long followed your work and been in hearty accord with the policies and plans which you have developed.

—PRESIDENT FRANKLIN D. ROOSEVELT, letter, 1934

The Maternity and Infancy Revolution

Edith Abbott
From "A Sister's Memories," ca. 1952, published in the
Maternal and Child Health Journal, 2004

On a hot Washington day in August 1921, my sister Grace Abbott officially became the highest ranking woman in the United States government, taking her place in the "temporary" make-shift wood-frame building which had been put up hastily during World War I to house the headquarters of the U.S. Children's Bureau.

The journalist Grace Phelps came to these offices while writing an article called "Grace Abbott, Mother of All of Uncle Sam's Children," and made an accurate sketch of what they were like. Miss Phelps wrote, "Down on the banks of the Potomac, near the stately Lincoln Memorial, there is a crumbling war-time building that is now being shored up to make it last another year or so. Too hot in the summer, dark and dreary in the winter, 'Tempo No. 5' houses one of the most important activities of the Federal Government—Uncle Sam's Children's Bureau.

"Insignificant as its exterior may be, and inadequate as its equipment is, visitors say that they find there an atmosphere of understanding and human sympathy that far transcends mere plaster-board walls. This, they say, is apparent at once in any contact with the all-too-limited personnel of the Bureau, and still more apparent in the chief of the Bureau, Grace Abbott."

Here it was that Grace arrived, to begin at once her work with the old and new problems that were left on the desk which had just been vacated by Julia Lathrop.[1]

The Children's Bureau had been created in 1912, by an act of Congress, and it had been directed to investigate and report upon "all matters pertaining to the welfare of children and child life among all classes of our people." It was the first public agency—not only in the United States, but in the world—given the responsibility to supply the facts with reference to the problems of child life as a whole.

It is hard to realize now what a revolutionary thing it was at that time to establish a Children's Bureau in a national government. In 1912 no other national government had such a bureau. The creation of the Children's Bureau was the first recognition that the national government had a responsibility to promote the welfare of the children of the nation, and it may be said to have ushered in a new and determining era in the child welfare movement.

From the creation of the Children's Bureau in 1912, there had been long, tedious denunciations of the Bureau as a revolutionary and socialistic measure. Socialistic? Not really. Revolutionary? Definitely. For the new Children's Bureau was not like the Department of Agriculture and the Interior, nor even the Bureau of Labor. As Grace explained, "All these older bureaus seemed to Congressmen to have a definite relationship to the production of wealth, which the government had encouraged from the beginning. [But] child welfare was different. It was either something sentimental and trivial—and therefore unworthy of interest on the part of the federal government—or, when advocated by men and women who were on record for the rights of workers, it was the expression of hostility to business interests and should not be allowed to get a foothold in Washington."

§

Grace's years at the Children's Bureau were filled with extraordinary experiences, but the most difficult and important responsibility that she faced in her first year as Chief of the Children's Bureau was the administration of the new Maternity and Infancy Act—the first system of Federal aid for social welfare in U.S. history. This act, usually referred to by the names of its Congressional sponsors as "Sheppard-Towner," was passed a few months after Grace went to Washington and gave the Children's Bureau the responsibility of administering a new Federal grant-in-aid to the states of $1,000,000 annually.[2]

In her work at Hull House Grace had more than thirteen years of first-hand knowledge of the helplessness of large numbers of women in trying to provide proper maternal and infant care. She had learned there about the neglect of maternity cases when she tried to improve the service given by midwives to immigrant mothers. The women dying unnecessarily in childbirth, or living afterward in chronic invalidism, was a very serious problem, and Grace looked to the Maternity and Infancy Act to give Federal leadership and Federal aid to the states, to help to prevent this neglect.

The maternity bill had become a campaign issue in the 1920 national elections, and prior to his election, President Harding announced his support for legislation adding, "It is for us a grim jest, indeed, that the federal government is spending twice as much money for the suppression of hog cholera as it spends for its entire program for the welfare of the American child."

Finally, the maternity bill passed the House on November 19, 1921, and the Senate at once acted to pass the amended House bill, which was signed by President Harding on November 23.

Grace was delighted but also a little frightened by her new responsibilities, for, during the Congressional hearings, there had been some disturbing previews of the resentment that many politicians felt toward the bill. As Grace wrote to our friend Sophonisba Breckinridge at that time, concerning the behavior of the Congress, "Dear Nisba, It is too ridiculous the way these grown men have behaved."

The Act, as finally passed, made provision for administration by the Children's Bureau of federal grants-in-aid to the states for the purpose of reducing maternal and infant mortality and to protect the health of mothers and infants.

The first job that supporters of the Act had faced, when rallying support for the Congressional battle, was to make the public realize that there were vast numbers of women and infants dying needlessly in this country, all because of ignorance. Simple instructions and rules of hygiene, easy and inexpensive to follow, were needed by mothers to protect their own health and the health of their children. The Children's Bureau had set about convincing the nation that a plan of public education, which would reach mothers in even isolated regions, was needed—and they had succeeded. Now, with the Act passed, came the much more difficult task of implementation.

The Act had been planned in the hope that some of the facilities and services that had been enjoyed by women in large cities would be made available in the rural areas, and Grace pointed out that the states must try to do their work "in the rural districts, among groups or classes of people in which the need was greatest."

Public health nurses soon appeared in all parts of the country—in counties where public health nurses had never been heard of before. In remote regions where even the postman was unknown, the maternity and infancy nurse "faithfully followed the trails to mothers and babies. On foot, on horseback, by automobile, by sleigh, she carries help and hope to countless homes."

Nurses visited the homes of infants and preschool children and expectant mothers, established health centers, organized conferences, promoted campaigns for breast feeding and for birth registration, assisted with immunization work, and organized talks, leaflets, motion pictures, and lantern slides.[3] Grace even developed plans to use the newly developed medium of radio broadcasting.

Grace explained, "The Children's Bureau does not want to print reports which the social historian might read some one hundred years from now and say the investigation was well made, and the recommendations valuable, and it was too bad nobody ever heard anything about it at the time the report was made. For this reason we have sought—by use of motion pictures, and by the popular press—to reach the public. Now that broadcasting by radio is possible, we recognize in it a new means of accomplishing this end."

In those pioneering broadcast days, there were still but few radios around the country, and re-broadcasting stations were still undeveloped, so the Bureau tried its first programs from the Navy station in Washington. As Grace recalled, "I went downtown to one of the few stores which then had receiving sets for sale, hoping to hear the talk. At my request to tune in the Navy station, the young man in charge of the demonstrations made a great effort to get the show. At last he gave it up, saying 'Well, lady, I finally got the station, but I'm sure this ain't what you want anyway. It's only some kind of a child health program.'"

People weren't yet used to radio, and they certainly weren't used to the radio being used as a means of social education. But Grace persisted, and for many years, over NBC and over CBS, the Children's Bureau sponsored regular weekly talks at times that Grace thought would be convenient for mothers.

Among its many other efforts to help, the Children's Bureau gave primary importance to the popular "child health conferences." To many communities around the nation, the coming of such a conference was heralded as "an event of greater interest to mothers and fathers than a transatlantic air flight!" Reports came to the Bureau of families who would pack lunch and start off, over mountains and plains, on an all-day trip to reach the doctor and nurse who had come to advise them.

The child health conferences were always directed by a physician, assisted by a state or county nurse. Children were examined, weighed, and measured, and mothers were instructed about the care of their children and told of physical defects which should be remedied. We take this kind of work so much for granted today that it is difficult to remember just how new and strange—how marvelous—it seemed to young parents back in the early 1920s.

Conferences were held in nearly all the states and in the thousands of counties. They were "held in grocery stores, churches, schoolrooms, homes." Sometimes an automobile clinic called the "Child Welfare Special" toured the countryside, taking up its stand on a tree-shaded lawn. "Babies of every race"—all were reached through these conferences.

Under the Act, 125,000 child health conferences were held, attended by a million and a half children. Over 2,000 permanent child health centers were established, many of which were later supported locally. Without question thousands upon thousands of young lives were saved through this effort.

Despite the great success of the work, however, always there were those in opposition. There were groups who feared any sort of government action as related to the family and spent much money and energy to bring the Maternity Act down.

Typical of their actions was a small pamphlet that one of them issued entitled, *Shall the Children of America Become the Property of the State?*, in which the authors described the Maternity Act as a "vile debauch of sacred rights," adding that "The Children's Bureau will by this Bill be the ruling power in the United States. This bureau, headed by one woman, will become the most despotic influence in the country."

When I first saw this booklet, I had to stop and marvel. Could that "one woman" really be my dear little sister, Gracie?[4]

FIVE

A Constitutional Amendment

Notes to Harold Cary for *Collier's* article, November 17, 1920[1]

You are shocked to discover that there are more than a million children between ten and fifteen years of age whom census enumerators recorded as "gainfully employed"; that this child labor is confined to no one section of the country, and to no single industry. You find this hard to reconcile with American concern for the welfare of children, and with sound principles of industrial organization. If we take a long view, there is definite progress to record. A hundred years ago, the introduction and development of the factory system in the United States was urged by statesmen because adult male labor, of which there was then a shortage, was not needed in factory work, and women and children—who would otherwise spend their days in "idleness" could be employed.[2] Philanthropists—there were no social workers in those days—added the argument that factories could give employment to orphans and "pauper" children who must otherwise "eat the bread of charity." The inventor sought to make machines that children from five to ten could operate.

Fifty years ago, the question of compulsory school attendance and, for that matter, of free public schools, was a subject of heated controversy. In 1873, six States had established a minimum age for factory work, and in four of these States, the minimum age was ten, in one, twelve, and in one, thirteen years. The hours these very young children were permitted to work was limited in fourteen States usually to a ten-hour day. This condition had been improved, but in some States in the U.S.—as in the countries of the Orient—it is still legal to employ a child of twelve to work ten hours a day.

Whatever our practices may be, our theories have changed. The employment of children, the Department of Commerce states, is not good business. Child welfare workers no longer say that the child who has suffered a loss in the death of a father or mother—which can never be made up to him—shall have the additional handicap of unequal education and the sacrifice of the good times that should go with childhood. We no longer apply the word "pauper" to children. Every State now has some kind of a compulsory education law, and developing tendencies in our child labor legislation are clear. The most advanced States require that a child shall reach an established age, educational, and physical minimum before he shall be allowed to go to work.

And yet there were, in 1920, more than a million working children—and only thirteen States which measured up to the standards of the Federal Law in every particular. Good laws are well enforced in a few States, and poorly enforced in others. And poor laws are also respected or scorned as the case may be. In 1916 Congress recognized the interstate character and obligations of the problem and passed the first Federal Child Labor Law. At that time, we set a new world standard and could hold up our heads among the nations of the world. That law and the Child Labor Tax Act have both been found to be unconstitutional, and most of the western civilized world has reached the mark which we then set.[3] But we do not intend to relinquish permanently first place among the nations of the world. We shall have to amend the Constitution so that State and Nation may together attack the problem of ensuring an approximation at least of equal opportunity for all American children.[4]

. . . As for State rights [as an argument against a Child Labor Law], I can conceive of any State being jealous of the right to establish higher standards for the protection of its children than the Federal Government may require; I confess I cannot understand any State being jealous of the right of individuals in the State to exploit the children of the State.

§

Who is opposed to the Amendment? I know of very few, and these can be put into three groups:

(1) Those who favor child labor. This may be the exploiting parent hard-driven by economic necessity, who cannot resist the temptation which an offer of employment to his child presents. One of the sad things connected with the recent industrial depression was that, sometimes, when neither the father nor mother could get a job, one could be found for the fourteen-year-old boy or girl whom they had hoped to see through high school. And reluctantly these parents put the child to work, and lived off his earnings while they walked the street looking for work.

(2) The employer who expects to win, not by efficient business organization, but by practices which other employers, with better industrial and humanitarian standards, will not resort to. All the people who, in one way or another, are dependent upon the favor of this child-exploiting employer join him in defense of child labor. These people, who want to keep children in the mills and the mines, do not say that they favor child labor, but instead they raise the question of State rights and local initiative in Washington, and at home they have other reasons which they urge for preventing the enactment or the enforcement of good State laws.

(3) Those who oppose any change in the U.S. Constitution, or any reduction of the reserved rights of the States. These people do not all favor child labor, nor do they all oppose it. There are other things which seem much more important to them than what happens to children. They are not always consistent. About a year ago, I listened to a prominent New York lawyer explain the importance of having law-enforcement in the hands of the local units of government, and the necessity of being patient with local communities in their apparent shortcomings. He said that, because he believed that

this was absolutely fundamental to our form of government, he did not favor a child labor amendment. During the next half hour, he was speaking in favor of a Federal anti-lynching law.

People are always opposed to Federal authority if they are opposed to, or indifferent to, the object for which Federal aid is sought. To some few, adherence to certain established forms seems more important than the very objects for which governments are established. In this last group are a few who have helped to secure better State laws for children, and, unfortunately for the children, they seem to have grown to like the crazy patchwork quilt of State laws which so unequally protects American children.

SIX

Public Protection for Children

From the National Conference of Social Work Proceedings,
June 1924[1]

I have chosen to speak tonight on the subject of public protection for children not because I have a new program to offer but because, first, public provision is so fundamental in a child-welfare program, and second, . . . legal and political questions which enter into such discussions have been frequently raised but little discussed in recent years.

. . . If we are to have . . . universal provision for all children . . . public aid must be enlisted. If a democratic community is committed to the policy of endeavoring to secure for all its children what the best and wisest parent wants for his own children, our efforts to realize this obligation must be continuous.

. . . Education and health offer . . . examples of some of the questions involved. . . . As soon as universal education instead of education of the few was accepted as a goal, free public schools became inevitable.[2] But they were not established without a struggle.

Those who opposed public taxation for education denounced its proponents as socialists, or as advocates of a dangerous kind of paternalism, but the complete answer was that universal education on any other basis was impossible. We have now a similar situation with reference to the health of children. If we set before us the ideal of reducing to the lowest possible level our present unnecessarily high infant mortality and of assuring real physical fitness for all children, public participation in the program becomes absolutely necessary. In its final analysis this is an extension of an educational program, for we look forward to making available for every father and mother and for every child information as to how to prevent disease and, of almost greater importance to parents, how to feed and clothe and train children so that they may know real physical and mental fitness as distinct from mere absence of disease.

In the face of some opposition and with more support we are going forward with this program. In every part of the country public programs are under way for promoting good prenatal care for mothers and scientific care for infants and for all children as they pass through the preschool and school periods and are later initiated into the working world. This may be denounced as socialized medicine, as the beginnings of state medicine, as a program supplied by Moscow, but to the real question: "Can the general health of children be safeguarded by any other method?" there is no answer.

§

Our political philosophy is grounded in fear. We have been taught that that government is best which governs least and that that government is least dangerous which is nearest to us. These are maxims which influence our thinking even though we do not accept them as true. Our history accounts in large measure for our belief in local responsibility; in social service it came not from our federal form of government, but by inheritance from England of the theory of parish responsibility for the poor of each parish.[3] Although local responsibility has behind it much sound political reasoning, in the United States as well as in England it has frequently furnished the explanation of neglect and of shameful incompetence and inefficiency. England's long struggle for centralized supervision began before our own. Ours has been won in discussion, but our practice still lags behind our theory in many parts of the continent.

It may help in some present controversies if we remember that although there has not been much objection in recent years to this process of state "centralization," as its opponents would call it, we owe that fact to the efforts of some who are here tonight and of others who belonged to an earlier generation of social reformers.[4] We do not today hear people saying that the abandonment of the county insane asylum, the county jail, or the county poorhouse is a direct blow at the foundation principle of local responsibility in government. It was, however, exactly so denounced when Dorothea Dix began her agitation for state and national provision for the insane.[5] Nowhere was this feeling of the importance of local government stronger than in Massachusetts, where Miss Dix began her work. But in the face of the facts which she presented, political theories had to give way, and Massachusetts took the first steps toward state care of the insane.

§

When it comes to the function of national government, there are new complications. I think all of you would agree that the very important field of research and general education as to established principles of child care is recognized as the province of the federal government.

The old theory that matters of national interest should be the function of the federal government and those which are purely local should be locally settled is still unquestionably the rule to follow. But what is national, what is state, and what is purely local becomes a question of fact rather than of political theory or political traditions. Those who are opposed to the particular undertaking under discussion can always be counted upon to talk much about the fundamental political principles involved and very little about the end which is sought. But there are a few who favor the object sought, to whom the political changes seem so dangerous as to warrant opposition. As I have already suggested, there were those who prophesied the fall of the Republic when it was proposed that new types of work should be taken over by the state and the authority of local governments was to be in any degree curtailed as well when a proposal to increase or develop national functions was made.

Although in many states local feeling has been as strong as state feeling, and geographic, economic, and social differences inside a single state are often as striking and as fundamental as the differences between any two states, this local community feeling has never been associated with a great struggle, and it finds expression in no familiar maxim which passes for thought and judgment.

Geographic relationship and economic and social conditions have all greatly changed. The most remote state may be nearer Washington in means of communication and transportation than Buffalo was to Albany or Boston to Springfield at the time the Constitution was adopted. Economic lines of development everywhere cross the arbitrary boundaries of the state. The industrial district of which New York City is the center crosses the boundaries of four states; that of Chicago, three states; while in the industrial districts of St. Louis, and many other cities, two states are included. The state in which an increasing number of men and women sleep and vote is not the state in which they work. We have come to recognize that local transportation problems of these and many other cities cannot be settled in either a single city or a single state. But the question as to whether education, health, or child labor present national problems is more frequently challenged.

That the welfare of children is a matter of more than local concern no one would challenge, since the future citizenship of the nation as well as of the individual state is always involved. Moreover, we have made a matter of national concern what has been happening to the children of Germany, Russia, Austria, and Armenia, as well as those of Belgium and Japan and Greece. Here in Canada, I may be reminded that most of the world has joined in an international effort to protect children.[6] There can be no question of the existence of a national interest in the protection of childhood. But there are always two questions, first, whether the need of national action exists, and second, whether further if the need exists it is at the time practical to meet the need by national action.

. . . Congress has not yet acted on the proposal of federal aid for general education, but that this proposal will be much discussed in the immediate future is clearly indicated.[7] It is important in the discussions that are to come that we keep close to the facts. Is there a national need and, as a matter of practical administration, can it be met in the way suggested? The same questions have been with us since 1781. The extreme states rights of the Articles of Confederation were promptly found to have a disastrous effect on business. From 1791 to the present, extensions of national authority which promoted commerce and agriculture have been made and will continue to be made as new conditions arise or as new understanding of old conditions develops. Extension in the social welfare field is therefore only a part of a developing tendency. We are not guided by the past in our social thinking. We cannot be guided by the past in the adaptation of political machinery to social needs not understood nor given recognition at the time that machinery was set up. We shall have to do our own thinking and assume responsibility for what we do or fail to do for the children of the present. Our political forefathers showed both courage and independence; our pioneers in social reform have lacked neither vision nor courage. I think no one of us prefers to forget our own responsibilities in satisfaction over the qualities that they displayed.

I cannot leave the question of public protection of children without saying something about the factor on which the success of any program depends—a properly qualified personnel. At the meeting of the Conference here in Toronto in 1897 in what was perhaps the most significant paper of all those presented, Mary Richmond discussed the need of a training school of applied philanthropy.[8] In it she set forth the imperative need of more and better training for the tasks which the social worker was undertaking to perform in the community and outlined with convincing concreteness the possible curriculum and the field of work. Although Miss Richmond's conclusions were challenged by some, it was only a short time before a beginning was made in meeting this new educational need. Today we have graduate and undergraduate schools giving general and specialized training. We have also, as I am sure all of you know, an organization of social workers which is trying to develop a professional attitude among ourselves and toward ourselves. There is, however, only one way by which these advancing standards can find permanent place in the public service, and that is through a recognition of the merit principle in appointment. The universal experience is that the merit principle is made certain in the public service by civil service and by civil service only.

. . . In many states and local communities, the civil service laws are badly drawn or poorly administered. This cannot be accepted as a reason for regarding civil service as a failure any more than we would advocate a return to employers' liability because a workmen's compensation law was badly drawn or administered. In the federal service we use now very commonly what is known as the non-assembled examination in which the applicant's education and experience are rated and an oral examination determines those qualities which only a personal interview can determine. I know of no better basis of choosing a properly qualified person than education, experience, and personal adaptation for the work. Under civil service all of the requirements for different types of service can be worked out as carefully as in the best-organized personnel bureaus; the only restriction on the civil service is that these standards once set up cannot be changed while the examination is in progress.

§

. . . Our history indicates that, as a rule, great steps forward usually come in a new community, or one in which the field has been so long uncultivated that it might be classified as virgin soil. The great advance the Middle West made in its provisions for education is a conspicuous example. Encouraged by a federal subsidy, for the first time in the history of the world a really comprehensive educational program was established. It supplemented the local elementary and secondary schools with free college, technical, and professional training and an extension service for the whole state and especially for the farmers. This program has become an integral part of the conception of public provision for education east of the Allegheny Mountains. All of this was done during the recurrent periods of agricultural depression and through the payment of taxes which involved greater sacrifices than the same provisions would have required in the richer Atlantic Coast states. It was based on what is the best conception of the reason for public provision and that is that the path of economy is co-operation of all the people in providing and in controlling the services which are in general needed by all. The heavily endowed school or agency does not exist in such communities; but it is one of the characteristics of frontier life that the people feel themselves adequate to the performance of any task of whose importance they have become convinced. And we hope that the frontier habit of thought is still ours and yours.[9]

SEVEN

Perpetuating May Day

From the *New York Herald Tribune*, May 5, 1929[1]

The first proclamation made by Mr. Hoover after he became President of the United States was that which he issued on March 25 setting May 1 as National Child Health Day, an occasion for "mobilizing the goodwill of the country toward childhood."[2] Today, which might be called National Child Health Sunday, that goodwill is being mobilized in our churches.

The President's proclamation was in accord with a joint resolution passed last year by Congress that May Day be annually dedicated to the happiness and health of children, thus giving official sanction to a five-year-old custom inaugurated by the American Child Health Association, of which Mr. Hoover for many years has been president.[3]

This yearly setting aside of a particular day to concentrate our national thought on the needs of childhood is an excellent thing, but its value evaporates into nothingness if on every day thereafter we settle back into an old routine of carelessness or ignorance, considering our duty done if one day annually is given to our children.

There have recently been introduced in Congress two bills whose aim is to continue throughout the year the spirit of May Day. . . . They provide for continuing the Federal aid given to the states for reducing the high national death rate of mothers.[4]

We are not only a wealthy, but a generous nation, and the latches of our pocketbooks fly open almost automatically when we hear the call of ignorance, disease, and suffering in any other country, especially when the call happens to be the pitiful cry of a child. . . . But the person who looks through glasses adjusted to a long-distance view is frequently blind to things right under his nose. Such, for a long time, was the case with this country. To a certain extent it is still the case.

At present, out of every 1,000 babies born [in the U.S.], sixty-five die before they are a year old, many of them sacrifices on the altars of ignorance and carelessness. In other words, their deaths are preventable by the application of present-day medical knowledge. There are other countries whose child conservation record is much worse than ours, but there also are others whose record is better—countries where babies have a better chance to grow to healthful manhood and womanhood than they would if they had been born citizens of the United States.

But painful as these unnecessary deaths of babies are to a land which has established a world-wide reputation for efficiency, our maternal death rate, among the highest of almost any civilized country in the world, should give us greater concern. There are no deaths more tragic than those of mothers in childbirth. American mothers in giving birth lay down their lives by the thousands every year—many of them victims of ignorance, disease, improper care, and even superstition.

On my desk as I write are letters and reports from health officers, nurses, field workers, and troubled mothers living in every state of the Union. Between the impressive business-like statements of facts and figures in official reports are occasional descriptions of specific cases, stories which reveal in blinding flashes how great is the need and the desire for help, education, and guidance.

Take this story, for instance, from North Carolina, in whose remote mountain cabins live the descendants of sturdy pioneers whom isolation has kept in amazing ignorance:

"Just recently," says the report, "a mountain girl in a neighboring county, thinking it took twelve months for a baby's full development, attempted to walk over a mountain to her relative, where she hoped to receive sympathy and care at term. Her baby was born in a cornfield, where a very small boy found her."

Mothers are less anxious about their own health than the health of their babies. The prenatal clinic is much less popular than the well-baby clinic. But the movement for safeguarding the health of mothers is gaining ground. The death rate has been started downward; particularly deaths preventable by adequate prenatal care are less frequent than formerly.

. . . It is not easy to estimate in dollars what return the country has received for the few millions spent from the National Treasury in this business of saving mothers and babies. Nor should we ever attempt such an estimate. The last available reports of the Vital Statistics Division of the Census Bureau show that in the birth registration area in 1927, approximately 24,500 babies lived who would have died if they had been born under the conditions which prevailed in 1922.[5] Of course, many agencies, both public and private, contributed to this happy result. But that the Federal Maternity and Infancy Act (Sheppard-Towner) and the nation-wide interest in child health which it created was an important factor all experts are agreed.[6]

After all, however, the number of babies kept alive is a very inadequate measure of the value of the joint services that have been set up during these seven years by the nation and the states. Not only have more babies lived than would otherwise have done so, but those who have lived are stronger and happier today because of the instruction their parents received from the doctors and nurses at the child health and prenatal conferences and through the many clubs and classes for mothers.[7]

EIGHT

The Next Steps

Speech given at the Twenty-Fifth Anniversary Conference
of the National Child Labor Committee, New York City,
December 16–17, 1929[1]

We look back tonight, not to celebrate the end of child labor—your
President has already told you of the work that lies ahead of you.
As a matter of fact, we meet at the end of this quarter of a century
of effort to take counsel together about the next steps that are to
be taken, because there always are those inevitable next steps in a
child welfare program.

I wish that I myself looked back over the whole twenty-five years of
service in this field. It is both a long period and a very, very short one
in the whole of the effort to emancipate children from the industrial
load that was put upon their shoulders. My own active participation in the movement began in 1917 with the enforcement of the
first Federal Child Labor Law, which this Committee had written
on the statute books with the help, let us say, of Congress and the
President.[2] At any rate, there it was to be enforced. It came at a very
difficult time, and I am pausing to speak of that because of the very
great help that Governor Roosevelt, then Assistant Secretary of the
Navy, was during that trying period. You remember we undertook
to enforce the first Child Labor Law just as the U.S. entered the
war, and the old kind of industrial patriotism seemed to be given a
new lease on life by being able to say that whatever they did was in
the interest of more effective production, and hence a means of
bringing the war to a victorious close. I remember one of my first
inspection trips was in the autumn of 1917, when we were anxiously

wondering in Washington why the coal never started from the mines, because there seemed to be a terrible coal shortage. I went into one of the West Virginia towns and found the tracks loaded with cars of coal which did not move, and at the office of the superintendent of a mine, I learned of a very tragic accident that had happened that very day. A boy under fourteen had been killed while working in one of the mines. His employment, of course, was contrary to both the Federal Child Labor Law and to the law of Virginia. The superintendent of the mines said to me, "Well, that boy, you know, Miss Abbott, died for his country."

There was a very awkward pause. I think he thought that I did not understand his definition of patriotism. And I was happy to be able to assure him the people in Washington who were responsible for the conduct of the War—the President and the secretaries and assistant secretaries of the Army and Navy—did not recognize that kind of patriotism either and that, at least in the autumn of 1917, they had not come to our last line of defense, and they had no intention of making the children the first line of defense as some people seemed eager to do.

. . . As we look back over twenty-five years we find that those who have worked in the field of child labor, who have been interested in the emancipation of the child from industrial exploitation, have inevitably been led to a consideration of all the problems of children. As you went about your work, you found a large number of people who believed that child labor was the inevitable accompaniment of low wages, of unemployment, of widowhood and orphanage, of schools poorly equipped to meet the needs of children restless under the old curricula that were intended to prepare for a classical course in college when their interests were in science, in engineering, in mechanics, in a life of action. To them child labor in the individual case and in the individual community seemed the way out of all these economic, social, and educational maladjustments.

"George" had to go to work because father did not get enough money to support the children, and "Mary" went to work because father had died and there were four younger children, and "John" would not stay in school because he hated school, and there was not anything there for him to do. . . .

But when society said, after all, child labor is not the remedy, not the way out, then we were faced with the necessity of deciding what we would do about all these problems. Some other method had to be found of caring for dependent children. The wages of father had to be increased, because we could no longer count on a family wage to meet family needs. Child labor was not to be the solution of unemployment. John would no longer be allowed to get a job when father was told there were no jobs. And the school must be remade, must be enabled to meet the needs not of a few children who are to go into professional life, but the needs of all kinds and sorts of children, good and bad and dull and bright. The child labor laws said, in effect: All children must be helped, by all the educational devices that can be discovered, to a richer, fuller life.

Anyone who has been interested in the child labor movement has encountered all of the problems of childhood. Here were the problems of health, or the neglect of health. Here were the problems of recreation or need of recreation. Here was delinquency and prevention of delinquency.[3] Here all our city problems and our rural problems were presented in the decision as to what should be done for the working child.

And so it is not surprising that the National Child Labor Committee—organized to strike at this one root of so much evil—should find itself interested in all the others.

. . . You will recall that one of the conclusions of the first White House Conference[4] was that there should be created in the Federal Government a Bureau that should be concerned with all the interrelated problems of childhood—indeed it was Miss Wald who has from the beginning, I believe, been a member of the Board of the National Child Labor Committee, who suggested it. The National Child Labor Committee, having learned by experience the National need for such an agency, took the leadership in presenting to Congress the reasons for the creation of the Children's Bureau. It was directed, as you know, to consider not just one aspect of the child, but all aspects of the child, to assist in discovering all the resources that there are in the community for advancing steadily the interests of children.

Whether that advance has been as rapid as you had hoped it might be, I cannot say. Whether in the future it will be as rapid as it ought to be is for groups like this to determine, because after all, what we do here in the United States for children is determined largely by how unselfishly a relatively small number will devote themselves to educating the public as to the needs of the child.

. . . We have, of course, a great challenge in the size and in the diversity of our country.[5] But we are all the children of pioneers. Those of us like myself who came from the Main Streets of the Middle West, or those of you who come from the great cities. We are still pioneering in industry, we are pioneering in international relationships, and in social relationships and the rights of childhood are fundamental rights which we must find ways of safeguarding.

And so, here tonight, all of us, I am sure are going to assure Dr. Adler[6] that with him we shall have no peace of mind, and no contentment until we have done for the children of America the things that we know need to be done—and have discovered and met needs that have not yet been revealed to us.[7]

NINE

Boarding Out

For Maurice Bisgeyer of the National Association of Jewish Centers,
Washington DC, November 6, 1930

All children are dependent. And all children are problem children.
But special provision must be made for those who are dependent
upon public or private assistance because of poverty, neglect, ill-
treatment, or abandonment by their parents, because they present
conduct problems which parents find themselves unable to deal with
or because they have some physical or mental handicap, requiring
such specialized care that parents of ordinary means and skill may
find themselves unequal to the task. Consideration of the cause and
prevention of dependency, whether individual, social, economic,
or political, should be recognized as a part of the responsibility of
those who undertake to administer a community program for the
treatment of dependency. But this paper is limited to a discussion
of only one aspect of treatment, that is, foster-home care. . . .

§

There is . . . general agreement among social workers today that no
child should be removed from his own home or from the custody
of his own parents or parent on account of poverty alone, or on account of illegitimate birth alone.[1] There is also general agreement
that no child should be permanently separated from his family
because of a condition necessitating temporary care away from
his home, and that care by relatives is, in general, to be preferred
to care by strangers. In other words, social workers now accept as
their first task the preservation of family ties, and social agencies

are prepared to spend money in keeping the child with his family instead of breaking it up.

This sounds like quite an elementary statement, but it has worked a revolution in the social treatment of dependency. Formerly there was money available to care for children away from their homes, but not to keep homes intact. To some extent this is still true. But now children who are dependent, merely because of the poverty of their parents or parent, are less frequently provided for away from their own homes. The greatest gain of the last ten or twenty years has been made in the provision for this group of children. Formerly the State or the private society said, in effect, to the child whose father had died and had not left sufficient [means] to care for his children:

"We are very sorry, of course, and we are prepared to help you. Our first step will be to make sure that, as you are now fatherless, you shall become motherless, too. We have built 'orphanages' for . . . you, and we will arrange for your prompt admission. It is more expensive for us to care for you in this way than it would be to assist your mother . . . and you should . . . appreciate our generosity. We do not intend that you shall forget the misfortunes that have come to you. You will live in a segregated institution, and dress differently from other boys and girls, so that in school or church or on the street your status will be recognized at once. You will, of course, find yourself handicapped when you begin life because you will not have the protection which a home gives. We will, therefore, arrange for you to begin your working life earlier than other boys and girls. Because you need it more than others, you will have less education than other children, but you will be taught to be clean and orderly and obedient and it is hoped you will grow up grateful to us, but hating to eat the bread of charity."

While it may still be done frequently, no social worker would undertake to defend a policy of removing children from their own homes solely on the ground of poverty, and it has been to prevent that from happening that the resources of the State in the form of mothers' pensions have been provided.[2]

TEN

The Challenge of Child Welfare

Speech given at the Annual Convention of the American National
Red Cross, Washington DC, April 14, 1931

I am very glad to have a chance this morning to greet the Red Cross
in national assembly.

. . . I am supposed to speak to you this morning about "The
Challenge in Child Welfare." I suppose that when a child is born
it is always a challenge to its parents and a challenge that must be
very seriously considered at many periods in its life.

I have been told that an English father always hopes that his son
will follow him. I think an American father always hopes that his
son will go further than he has gone, and he lays his plans with
that objective. The American mother hopes the same thing for the
child, however loyal she may be to what her husband has done, or
what she has tried to do. Each generation with us is supposed to go
ahead of the past generation. Our hope always has been that the
America of the future is to be a very different America from the
America of the present.

But we have at this moment very special challenges in regard to
children in the United States.[1]

We have just spent, under the leadership of the President, a very
considerable amount of time and money in a canvass of what needs
to be done for children, what we are now doing to meet those needs,
and what still remains to be done.

If you read the reports of the White House Conference when
they appear, you will find that all kinds of expansion of public and

private undertakings were recommended as necessary if we are to meet the challenge of American children. For the challenge that comes to us is that we should live up to the knowledge and the opportunity that are ours—of putting into practice what we now know can be done for children in the way of preventing disease, delinquency, and dependency. That means a large undertaking, for our knowledge greatly transcends our performance.

. . . Since the industrial depression we have had to have the same type of expansion in general public relief for families. In the reports that come to the Children's Bureau, which were assembled at the request of the President's Committee on Employment, we find that in seventy-five out of one hundred cities reporting, 72 percent of the total family relief funds last year was given out of the public funds, out of taxation. Public relief grants increased nearly 150 percent in 1930 over 1929, while private relief increased 48 percent.

We are, therefore—I say "we" again because it is all of us who are responsible for the public relief—engaged in a joint public enterprise, trying to do the best that we can to meet the present emergency. What the public does, you do also, because you are citizens before you are members of the Red Cross. If it is not well done, that is your responsibility, and this year it is an immediate responsibility to have it well done. Now I am aware that it is harder to influence standards of public relief than to insure that what you are doing through the Red Cross is well done. But at the present moment local public relief is so important in the prevention of suffering that it seems to me a special responsibility lies on all those who understand relief of seeing that it is all well done.

. . . The Red Cross has made it difficult for us to sleep when children were hungry in any part of the world and has brought to us the challenge of helping them in many countries. I hope it will also help in bringing to us that same discomfort if children are hungry anywhere in the United States. We rely upon it to help us know where they are, as well as to help in whatever plan of organization for relief may seem to be necessary.

We are being asked whether we will live up to the gospel that we have been preaching of what constitutes an adequate diet for children. It will be very hard to live up to it always, and we may fail sometimes—but we must then honestly admit our failure. . . . The challenge of children is, then, always a challenge of very peculiar immediacy. I think people believe very often that I am impatient, but impatience is necessary where children are concerned.

I have stated again and again that the only time we can save the babies who are going to die this year, is this year. If we wait until next year, they will be dead. The only time we can care for children in any particular period of life is now. If a school child does not get what he needs, he will permanently bear the effect of that lack. If you postpone assistance until a more convenient time, you postpone it indefinitely as far as that child is concerned, and the result will be a permanent marring of the physical development and of the mental life of the child because of the period of neglect. You and I can go without a great many things and probably be better off, but in the case of children, this is not so. Yet one finds again and again the feeling that these services for children can be curtailed. I remember just ten years ago in the autumn of this year, when the Conference on the Reduction of Armament, which President Harding called was meeting in Washington. We were then also in the midst of an industrial depression. I was feeling very unhappy, because almost every place I went, the agencies for children were threatened with reduction of budgets and almost every report I read showed that this had happened. I remember saying to one or two of the people that I talked with, distinguished foreign visitors, that it was a very hard year for us, and children's work would probably be curtailed. I was greeted with so much astonishment, that in the midst of such wealth as the United States had I could be talking like that, that I never ventured to speak of it to foreigners again. I know and you know that, in spite of the handicap in 1921 and 1931, we are a tremendously rich people, full of vigor and enthusiasm as to what the future holds for us, and convinced that it rests in the hands of the children of today. What we do to them is going to determine not only the future of the United States, but to a large extent, the future of the world. Children mean self-sacrifice for any family which does for children the things that need to be done. Even in the richest family, unless the father and mother make great personal sacrifices, the children are going to be much neglected, since they will be handed over to hired people for care of every kind. So in all families—in the richest and even more in the poorest families, children require the sacrifice of personal convenience.

It is not always the richest family that meets this challenge the most successfully. Sometimes wealth gets in the way of proper consideration for children. It is not always the rich community that does the best for its children, unless it is prepared to sacrifice intelligently to see that the needs of the children are met. Intelligent sacrifice, so far as Americans are concerned, means that we accept the challenge, not only of the Philippine children with their increasing tuberculosis, or Puerto Rican children and those of our other far-flung possessions, but also the challenge of those who are very near at home in individual families and communities, and that we will make sure that the affection and interest and eagerness to do for them what should be done, will be expressed, and fully expressed, in our planning and care for children.

ELEVEN

The Real American Vice

Speech given at the Conference of State and Provincial Health
Authorities of North America, April 29, 1931[1]

Instead of reading a formal paper on the subject of the "Future
Plans for Protection of Maternity and Infancy," I am going to do
what I think will be more profitable—discuss quite informally what
seems to be the present outlook for continuing and expanding our
maternity and infancy and general child health program. . . .

In this whole problem of the promotion of health of mothers and
children, we have our past experience to build on. It is not a very
long experience, for it is only relatively recently that we have had
a specialized organization having this end in view. Sometimes the
movement is said to have begun with those first milk stations that
were established by Nathan Strauss in New York City in 1893.[2] . . .

The date which we think of in connection with public organization for meeting the special needs of children is 1908, when the
first child-hygiene bureau in a department of health was established
in New York City under the direction of Dr. S. Josephine Baker.[3]
Its organization was a recognition of the fact that the problem of
safeguarding the health of children is different from the problem
of safeguarding the health of the population as a whole, and that
special organization, special training and a special program are
therefore necessary to meet the needs of the young part of our
population.

. . . Promotion of maternal hygiene entered the field of public
health even later than child hygiene. The first organized effort to

provide prenatal care to expectant mothers was begun in 1908 in New York City by the Association for Improving the Condition of the Poor and the pediatric department of the New York Outdoor Medical Clinic.[4] . . .

When the Children's Bureau was established in 1912, the relation between early infant deaths and conditions associated with prenatal and delivery care was well recognized. As Chief of the Children's Bureau, Miss [Julia] Lathrop began her work for children with the prenatal period, and from that time to the present the Bureau has had as its objective the whole child and has continued to keep the importance of adequate care for the mother before the public. Its first bulletin for mothers and one of its earliest publications was on prenatal care. . . .

The Maternity Center Association of New York City came into existence in 1918 and did much to arouse national as well as local interest by reports of the results of its demonstrations.[5] Some of the municipal health departments then began to emphasize the importance of prenatal care, but no State department of health developed what could be called a maternal-hygiene program until after the passage of the Maternity and Infancy Act in November 1921, nine years ago.[6] State departments of health then undertook to promote the health of the child from conception, and the education of the public in the fundamentals of maternal hygiene began on a national scale. To the State divisions of maternal and child health fell the difficult task of educating the public, and particularly women, in the essentials of good prenatal and maternal care.

You will recall why it was difficult. Mothers quick to respond to suggestions for better care for the baby were slow to act in what seemed to be solely their own interest. There were some States in which it was not good form to speak of the prenatal period of childhood and the causes of the deaths of mothers in childbirth. How those deaths could be prevented was not considered a subject for consideration by either the general public or prospective parents. There were States in which the Children's Bureau film, *Well Born*, could not be shown because its general theme was held to be included in those prohibited by the censorship law. The initial period of the work was necessarily influenced by this general attitude. The whole program had to be approached by indirection. The inauguration of prenatal letters, of correspondence courses in maternal care, of the enrollment of midwives in classes, and demonstration of the work of a prenatal center has laid the foundation for a more effective program.

. . . Now when we are here together we ask what about the future of the work? . . .

There may be some who still think public money should not be expended for special maternal and infant hygiene services. There are some who think the health of children can take its turn with malaria or venereal-disease control in the general health program. They would have the State services and the local services in the child health field reduced to a minimum. This is not, I believe, the viewpoint of any of the specialists in child health nor the viewpoint of the general public. I have read recently an article by Dr. Ernest Caulfield in the *Annals of Medical History* on the beginnings of the infant-welfare movement in the eighteenth century.[7] The reluctance of physicians at that time to undertake the care of sick children and the fact that really distinguished physicians discouraged George Armstrong, the first pediatrician, on the ground that there was "nothing to be done for children when they are ill" is of interest in this connection. There are those who feel the same about the child-health movement today. But there are also those who realize that the child is not a pocket edition of the adult, and that planning for the whole child is necessary for optimum gains. . . .

The real American vice, I think, is that we get an idea, carry it out in a few places, find it is useful, and then think the job is done over this vast country of ours. I am sure if anyone were to ask you, when you were traveling in Europe, whether we have, let us say, juvenile courts in America, you would say, "Oh yes, we had the first in the world; we have them all over the country."[8] As a matter of fact, while these courts originated in the U.S., not half of the population of the country is served by specially organized juvenile courts. The rural and small-town population cannot be said to be so served. What would be the reply in relation to child-health centers?

In all our "social services," if you use those words as the English do to include education, health, and public social work, we have hardly begun to organize for adequate services throughout the States.[9] It is the function of the State departments both in health and in welfare, to see that these services are scientifically organized and available throughout the States. The report read by Dr. Palmer at the last session of the White House Conference, gave us some measure of the extent to which our program—that every child should be examined and under medical supervision—has been realized. We have formulated an ideal, we have interested a certain part of the public in each economic group, but we have hardly made a beginning in the realization of health services for all American children. There are new groups of mothers each year; new methods of safe-guarding children and new methods of child trainings are being developed. The child-health work needs to be put on a permanent basis, to be carried on year in and year out, season after season. It requires intelligence and ingenuity to present it so as to keep the public interested and to increase constantly the numbers of children and mothers who are reached—and at the same time to improve the character of the service rendered them. . . .

The responsibility of the Children's Bureau is to bring to public attention, in-season and out, the needs of children. Considered as part of the general population, children do not get the attention they should have. We can serve children adequately without sacrificing the needs and interests of the other population groups. But if the interest of one must be sacrificed, shall it be children?

It is time I closed. Before doing so, I want to say that I appreciate very much the courtesies that the Children's Bureau has always had at the hands of the State health officers and the cooperation you have given us whenever we have asked your help for any piece of work we were undertaking in your jurisdiction. If it has seemed to you that we sometimes pushed when you did not want us to push, and have perhaps elbowed our way in when it seemed to you that a lady ought to stay in the background, I can only say I am sorry. Unfortunately, we may still have to do some pushing and shoving to get the necessary attention for the needs of children. I promise you we shall be just as ladylike about it as we can; and when we cannot be properly ladylike, you will, I think, know that the pushing and shoving is sometimes forced upon us.

TWELVE

The Washington Traffic Jam

Speech given upon receiving the Gold Medal of the National
Institute of Social Sciences from Homer Folks, secretary of the
State Charities Aid Association of New York, May 7, 1931[1]

. . . Mr. Folks . . . is quite right, I think, in indicating that there is
no one in Washington that has been given a more important job
to do than has the Chief of the Children's Bureau, although she is
not so ranked in the news of the day nor in the list that is prepared
with such exactitude and so many flutterings—the official social
list of Washington.[2]

The fact that the Bureau is young—one might almost call it a
child among Government bureaus—may be the reason why it has
not received in its appropriation and other evidences of success and
esteem, the position that has come to some of the other Bureaus.[3]
But there are perhaps other explanations than its youth.

Sometimes when I get home at night in Washington, I feel as
though I had been in a great traffic jam. The jam is moving toward
the Hill where Congress sits in judgment on all the administrative agencies of the Government. In that traffic jam there are all
kinds of vehicles moving up toward the Capitol. There are all the
kinds of conveyances, for example, that the Army can put into the
street—tanks, gun carriages, trucks, the dancing horses of officers,
and others which I have not even the vocabulary to describe. But
they all finally reach the Hill, and they make a plea that is a very
old plea—one which, I find, in spite of the reputation for courage
that they bear, men respond to rather promptly. The Army says to
them, "Give lest you perish"; and fear as a motive is still producing

results on a scale which leaves the rest of us feeling very envious of the kind of eloquence the Army and Navy can command.

But there are other kinds of vehicles in this traffic jam—great numbers of them which, coming from Nebraska as I do, do not seem to me to get the attention they should as they move down the streets. These are the hayricks and the binders and the ploughs that the Department of Agriculture manages to put into the streets. When the drivers get to the Hill they have an argument which Congressmen understand. They say to them when they ask for appropriations for research in animal husbandry, "Dollars invested on this side of the ledger will bring dollars in geometrical or arithmetical progression"—depending on the enthusiasm with which they speak—"on the other side." And if there is one thing that a Congressman, and for that matter people in general, understand it is a balance on the profit side of the ledger; and when the drivers of these agricultural vehicles demonstrate that they will be able to show a balance on the profit side, there is a very generous appreciation of their argument.

Then, there are other vehicles. The handsome limousines in which the Department of Commerce rides. . . . To be sure, the limousines are looking a little bit shabbier this year, and their drivers are not speaking with quite so much assurance when they get to the Hill as they did in former times. But they still have a very convincing argument to make. They tell the Appropriations Committee that if a young man is sent to this town in Africa or that town in China or some place in Europe, American exports will at once begin to flow to that town and the returns are again going to demonstrate that expenditures for the Bureau of Foreign and Domestic Commerce are a real investment, yielding large returns to American business; so they, too, come away with a very good return for the effort they make in getting up to the Hill.

I am not going to describe all the vehicles in this traffic jam tonight. I am not going to tell you about the barouches in which the Department of State rides with such dignity, or the noisy patrol in which the Department of Justice officials sometimes appear. Without my saying more you will agree that it seems to be a traffic presenting special hazards. It seems so to me as I stand on the sidewalk watching it become more congested and more difficult, and then—because the responsibility is mine and I must—I take a very firm hold on the handles of the baby carriage and I wheel it into the traffic.

There are some people who think it does not belong there at all. There are some who wonder how I got there with it and what I think I am going to be able to do. And there are some who think the baby carriage is the symbol of bolshevism instead of the symbol of the home and the future of America.[4]

. . . When I get to the Capitol after much difficulty and begin to state the case for the Children's Bureau, I discover a serious handicap. Those men in Congress are really just as fond of children as I am. They are fond of their own children and their friends' children, but they are usually not familiar with what is happening to many American children, and they often lack the imagination to translate the facts and figures which are presented to them in terms of actual children.

I suggest to them that money invested on one side of the ledger brings—what? Well, we can show results, but how shall we measure these results? What is the life of a baby worth? What shall we put down as the value of the life of a mother?

. . . There are statisticians who have tried to figure out what those things are worth, but I have never found these statistical estimates very helpful. They have tried to determine the life-value of a man or a woman. They arrive at the conclusion that a man is worth very much more than a woman, since the test of worth is earning capacity, and as most mothers are not wage-earners, they must be rated at zero in this scale of values. You and I understand these human values, and we know that they cannot be expressed in that commonly used denominator of value—money. For this reason it is difficult to state the relation between the expenditures recorded on one side

of the national ledger and the results as expressed in terms of better health and better social outlook for children. We have learned
that the value of an educated citizenship cannot be estimated in
dollars, and the public is gradually coming to an understanding of
the value of the newer social services.[5]

THIRTEEN

Why Did Child Labor Ever
Develop in America?

From the Abbott Papers, University of Chicago, ca. 1933

In signing the Cotton Textile Code, the first to be agreed to under the National Recovery Act, President [Franklin] Roosevelt declared that the prohibition of the employment of children under sixteen years of age which it maintained was "one of the outstanding points in a new era of American business."[1] . . . One wonders why it should have been so long in coming? Why, indeed, child labor ever developed in democratic America.

The economic history of the U.S. reveals that at about the same time that Robert Owen was writing his tracts against the employment of young children in factories, Alexander Hamilton, the Secretary of the Treasury of the U.S.—who is so frequently used as a measuring rod of the greatness of those who have followed him in that high office—was advocating the employment of little children in the mills, whose establishment he was urging should be by a protective tariff.[2] The great capitalists of that day were the landlord, who hesitated to support a policy which, by creating a new demand for labor, would jeopardize the labor supply for agriculture in our sparsely settled country. Hamilton had a ready answer. Adult men, he said, in his famous report on manufacturing, were not needed in a machine equipped factory; women and children of eight and ten "who would otherwise be idle" could be used as operators in the textile mills. He was right. The machinery which came from England for what was then truly an infant industry, was especially built to accommodate little children. The regulation of child labor in this country was delayed not because the leaders in social reform were converted to the ruthless industrial patriotism of Hamilton, but because of the absorbing struggle over the abolition of slavery and the problems of reconstruction [that] followed the Civil War[, which] delayed the development of the whole social reform movement in America. Labor Unions secured a few laws, which generally went unenforced in Connecticut, Massachusetts, and New York before 1860, but the real child labor movement did not get underway until the last decade of the nineteenth century.

. . . A century ago the hours in a textile mill were from six in the morning until eight at night during ordinary times, and in rush periods from three in the morning until ten at night, and the children who worked these long hours were often as young as seven and eight. Legislative committees found that many of them had literally to be driven to go to work, or to keep it up after they were there. I have the same feeling of unreality as I read the official reports—of little children of six and seven working in the dark in mines, harnessed to coal cars to drag them through small openings; of the chimney sweeps or "climbing boys" compelled to go up the chimneys by beatings and under whom fires were sometimes lighted when they became frightened and refused to climb—as I had about the cruelties with which the fairy tales of my childhood were filled. And yet, long after these practices were exposed, and after law was passed prohibiting them, the practices continued.[3]

FOURTEEN

Promoting the Welfare of All Children

Speech given at the Children's Bureau Dinner,
Washington DC, April 8, 1937

It was thirty-five years ago that Miss Wald and Mrs. Kelley had a vision of a national service for children and set out to tell others of the light they had seen.[1] Miss Wald persuaded people of the usefulness of a Children's Bureau; Mrs. Kelley spurred them to action by a recital of the wrongs from which children suffered. It is not possible to name all those who helped in the ten-year campaign which preceded the passage of the Act creating the Bureau. . . . But in spite of all the thought that went into the development of the plan for the Bureau, the appreciation of a unified study of the interrelated problems of the child, the Bureau would have meant little or nothing except for the fact that President Taft announced that politics would not be a consideration in the appointment of the chief of the Bureau.[2] . . . [W]hen he discovered that in the opinion of those who were deeply interested in the success of the Bureau, Julia Lathrop was the person best qualified to head the Bureau, Mr. Taft took what many regarded as a bold and dangerous step and became the first President to appoint a woman to a major executive position in the Government. Miss Lathrop, by attacking the fundamental problems of childhood in a scientific way, established a tradition which the Bureau has sought to maintain from that time to the present. We have been pilgrims following a vision. . . . While our legislative mandate was to promote the welfare of all the children of all the people, we have had to seek out especially those in greatest need—for the announced objective of this Government is equality of opportunity for its children. We have, therefore, known the mean streets better than the boulevards; the Delectable Mountains and the Enchanted Mound were not for us.[3] We have not the applause of the G-men, nor the social position of those who serve the government in the State Departments.

Historically, the children or the cause of children has been the spearhead in the struggle for better economic and social conditions, better organization of the government for the services of its citizens. The bitter fight of a century ago for the regulation of the employment of children was the beginning of labor legislation. It was stubbornly fought for exactly that reason. Cure, rather than punishment, as an objective in the treatment of crime was first tried for children. Resources for the supervision of the health of children have preceded those for adults. This fact—that those who have undertaken to safeguard children must propose what often seems, at the time, a revolutionary change in the conception of the functions of government, and must experiment with new administrative and judicial procedures—requires a combination of courage and wisdom, of sagacity and opportunism, of patience and of impatience if results are to be achieved.

In a federal agency, successful national leadership has depended upon state and local cooperation. The Children's Bureau has known that all wisdom did not reside in Washington; that constructive and creative leaders could be found in state and local government. We have appreciated the great services that the private agencies have rendered—but it has also been clear that if the needs of all children were met, the public treasury must pay the bill.

. . . This problem of the relationship of the several levels of government presents difficulties. The Bureau has always believed in the method of conference, in intellectual honesty in dealing with the states, but has maintained at the same time that its responsibility could not be evaded.

. . . While victory for the cause of children is sweet, defeat we know can only be temporary. The friends of children command the future. Those who have resisted their forward march have left a record in history that their descendants read with embarrassment. So I am sure it will be with those timid individuals and institutions who are afraid to trust Congress—fearful of democratic government—who are willing children should continue to be exploited lest some fantastic evils might result.

There is, of course, nothing more important in a democracy than that the welfare of not a few children but of all children must be considered. That struggle to secure their rights and meet their needs must continue. If the Children's Bureau is to meet the hopes of those who are responsible for its creation, it must continue the strenuous life. There is no life of ease ahead. . . . The accomplishment of one objective only makes more obvious the need of pressing on to the next.

FIFTEEN

Children and the Depression

From *From Relief to Social Security*, 1941

Babies do not thrive in institutions, and in normal times it would be possible to find foster homes for such babies, but the private agencies have not been able to assume the care of these young children because their funds have been inadequate.

The extent of the need has discouraged some communities and individuals from doing what they could in the emergency. It has led others to seek escape by flight from responsibilities they assumed long ago. Legislatures have adjourned without making the necessary provision for the board of the children accepted by a state agency in accordance with a state law. Collectively, the people of these states were in the same class as deserting fathers.

§

. . . It is important not to forget that, in the long future, our democracy will have to pay in perhaps arithmetical or even geometrical progression for our failure to bring security and stability to the care of these especially disadvantaged children. Society will pay eventually for its failure, also, to provide for foster care for children now being cared for in demoralized homes on emergency relief; for not making longtime plans for the forlorn youngsters left stranded through one cause or another who are now being cared for in the home of this or that relative who is receiving unemployment relief and finding it inadequate for the needs of his own children.

Whatever the plight of the children of the unemployed may be, these other children whose fathers are dead or whose parents are worse than dead are peculiarly unhappy, neglected members of society. The community will, of course, care for them after some fashion. But we have studied the end results of poor, haphazard care sufficiently to know the costliness of the failure to meet the needs of these children adequately.

§

You will remember that before the depression, in the days of our noisiest and most offensive national self-confidence, there were great numbers of children who were condemned to endure serious handicaps—physical, intellectual, and social—because of the economic conditions to which they were born.

I can make this concrete by a few illustrations. In the days before 1929 as you were coming into almost any city in the United States on the railroad, you passed through areas in which the houses were clearly unfit for human habitation. If it were your home city and you had with you friends who were just making its acquaintance, you may have had some regrets that the railroad approach went through so unattractive a part of the city, and, as you whisked them away to a section where pleasant homes and attractive surroundings were the rule, you hoped they would forget, as you were in the habit of forgetting, those ramshackle little houses, those ugly and overcrowded tenements and streets. We have all done this. We still do it.

Children have always lived under these conditions. Most of us are sorry, but our sympathy, our sense of responsibility for community conditions, has been short lived and unproductive. Most of us, if we had thought at all about these tenements with their crowded homes, did not accept this as a problem which we must solve. Such conditions have seemed to many of us an inescapable part of our social life. But you, who are young and eager for service, must not accept such conditions as inevitable. They can be changed now, and we owe it to the future not to forget or to ignore the handicaps which such homes place on the children who occupy them.

We shall find it necessary to begin by acknowledging that the income of the lowest wage-earning groups in the United States has never been large enough to pay a rental sufficient to make it possible for them to rent decent, comfortable homes in a favorable environment.

. . . Housing is not the only problem. Health—perhaps the most important of all gifts to children—has been largely determined by economic conditions. . . . A few years ago the editor of the leading medical journal of the country said at a meeting of the American Medical Association that people got the kind of medical care they could afford to pay for, just as they got the kind of motor car or rug; and he apparently considered this a complete reply to criticism of unnecessary deaths and invalidism. He expected the haphazard system of individual medical charity to continue. We all acknowledge that such charity helps some children, but surely we agree in thinking that it is wholly inadequate as a health program.

. . . How are we to insure to children that inalienable right to health and physical vigor that should be their birthright? I realize this is not an easy question to answer. It raises many questions about which there is some disagreement. Unquestionably a nation-wide program for making available to parents the services of child-health centers is greatly needed, and to this there should be no opposition. . . . It is clear that we must repudiate the theory that health is in the same category as rugs or motor cars. And we must accept as a first principle the doctrine that the interest and welfare of children and of society must be our test of what we shall or shall not do.

§

It may well seem important that I should not finish without an apology. . . . But I do not apologize. Injustice and cruelty to children are as old as the world. We have made some progress. We see things more clearly now than in the past; and with clearer vision we can do more, go farther.

Without apology, then, I ask you to use courageously your intelligence, your strength, and your goodwill toward children in the progressive removal of the economic barriers which have retarded the full development of children in the past. There will, I warn you, be discouragements and disappointments. But the cause of children must always triumph ultimately. New standards of what constitutes scientific care and new knowledge as to what are the social needs of children will develop. The important thing is that we should be "on our way" toward adequately meeting their needs. Perhaps you may ask, "Does the road lead uphill all the way?" And I must answer, "Yes, to the very end." But if I offer you a long, hard struggle, I can also promise you great rewards. Justice for all children is the high ideal in a democracy. It is the special responsibility of women. We have hardly, as yet, made more than a beginning in the realization of that great objective.

PART III

Women

I have not as yet said anything about the death of Miss Grace Abbott, but I feel that I want to pay a tribute to one of the great women of our day. No one who knew her could help but admire and respect her. It is with sorrow we see pass from the stage a woman of this type, for we have lost a definite strength which we could count on for use in battle.

—ELEANOR ROOSEVELT, newspaper column "My Day,"
June 23, 1939

How Women Achieve in Government

Frances Perkins
A tribute, from *The Child*, August 1939[1]

Grace Abbott I regard as one of the greatest women we have ever produced in the United States of America. Perhaps the best answer I could give to a question of "how women attain real achievements in government" is to say why and how Grace Abbott achieved in government. She held high office in the Federal Government as Chief of the Children's Bureau, and she could have held higher office if she had desired.

. . . What was her pattern? First of all, it was a pattern of professional standards and perfection . . . of competence: the same competence and skill that a craftsman has, or a machinist has. She knew how to do. She knew how to analyze social problems. She knew where to find the medication or the relief for these problems; she knew how and when to apply it; and she knew and understood the human heart and the human brain through which it had to be applied.

Grace Abbott had knowledge. She studied to get knowledge; then she went on and kept her power of acquiring more knowledge out of experience and out of other people's experience. That, of course, is one of the great advantages of the trained and educated mind—it can learn not only by its own experience, but by the recorded experience of others, and learn to associate these two phases of developing information into one pattern.

The old-fashioned virtues of conscience and character were hers. The advance of women in government or in the learned professions is impossible without conscience and character. Women without those qualities—however brilliant their minds may be, however sparkling their personalities—will not make the progress that we want to see them make.

Grace Abbott had that broad cultural education which expanded the heart and strengthened the faith and aspiration; she had professional training which sharpened her mind as a tool; and she had that self-discipline which everyone needs who undertakes a responsibility. Everyone who takes an oath and solemnly swears to perform certain duties "under the law and within the law, so help him God," must impose upon himself a certain self-discipline, and persons who have not learned self-discipline as early at least as their years of education find it hard to acquire under later stresses and strains when they bear responsibility.

Then, Grace Abbott had a profound and steady and unalterable unselfishness: She had always the conception that she was less important than the people whom she served, than the women and children of this country who looked to her for the solution of their troubles. I knew her once to risk her health against the plea of all of us, for we were worried about her health. Her only answer was, "No person is as important as this program which we have in mind, and it so happens that for the moment I am the only person who can defend it. The rest of you can stay outside and shout, and that will help. But because I am the only person who can defend it, to be of help to mothers and of help to infants, to save infant lives and maternal lives, I am the one to go forward and fight for it." She went with the most extraordinary disregard of herself—what I call truly scientific and impersonal unselfishness.

Her ability to cooperate enabled her to work with all kinds of people. It is one of the greatest assets which every woman who, like Grace Abbott, undertakes to go into public life and public office must learn—the art and the grace of humility. I have seen her—and she was a proud woman—with great humility suffer fools gladly, listen to the most preposterous advice respectfully; and, if it was kindly and warm-hearted, she thanked the giver for the advice and that, of course, was done with real sincerity. That was why she was able to cooperate with all kinds of people and get the best out of them. Nobody ever got so much work out of any staff, I think, as she did, and that was because she knew how to cooperate with people, not only how to direct them, but to bring out the best that was in them.

Her manners were what I like to call "equalitarian manners." I remember being taught by my father as to what were the proper manners for people who lived in a democracy—how one must never overlook any one, because the least of these is our brother and, in addition to that, our fellow citizen; and how one must have a way, an approach to people with whom one talked, not subservient, not arrogant—I know no better word for it than equalitarian. That does not mean to have rough manners. They are good manners, manners of dignity and kindness. Grace Abbott had those, and every woman who hopes to go into public office must learn to acquire them. There must be no pride of intellect, no pride in experience, and no pride like vanity if women are to do the work that they have the opportunity to do in high public office.

And then she had the capacity to take ridicule and abuse (I have seen her do it) without anger or resentment or—more important—a sense of degradation or despair. Many remember the days when speeches were made on the floor of Congress asking what right that "old maid" had to go to people and tell them how to bring up their children! Grace Abbott and her predecessor, Julia Lathrop, had to "take it," but they walked out smilingly, just as though nothing had happened.

Because she had flexibility, Grace Abbott could change her mind and adapt her program, was ready to take the best she could get at the moment and go forward from what she had to what she believed ought to be.

In short, Grace Abbott had the qualities and virtues that I think will help women to be successful in the administration of government enterprises of all sorts—for those who administer government enterprises deal with the public. The public must be met on honest grounds in an honest way, yet with full insight into the problem and into the meaning of the problem, and into the agony and the tragedy of those who hope the Government will help them solve their particular problems.

. . . One of the tasks of the educated woman is to help make the relationship among all our people one of confidence and sympathy and understanding, not because one has read about trouble in books, but because, like Grace Abbott, one has known and seen poverty and allowed one's self to be touched by it and its pity and terror.

The example of Grace Abbott's life and work is worth following—insight developed by direct contact with poverty and trouble. She summoned her knowledge, her skill, her discipline, and found the practical solutions. She summoned her courage and her patience and applied adroitly the solutions to the situation.

SIXTEEN

Dorothea Dix

Speech given at the Biennial Convention, General Federation
of Women's Clubs, Atlantic City, May 27, 1926

. . . Is there a technique to be followed in securing social legislation? . . . For the sake of perspective I should like to go back nearly
a hundred years to consider the methods of Dorothea Dix because
her method of work and the obstacles she encountered are of special interest at this time. Born in 1802, her humanitarian career
did not begin until she was nearly forty—older for that time than
at present.

In 1841 a chance visit to the East Cambridge jail to teach a Sunday
class of twenty women prisoners started Dorothea Dix on her humanitarian career. Among the prisoners she found a few insane,
confined in an unheated room on the theory that heat was unnecessary for those suffering from a mental disease. Failing in her efforts
to persuade the jailer to provide heat and make the insane in his care
more comfortable, she at once took the case to the court, and heat
was supplied by order of the judge. Although she was so frail that
her friends had argued that she was not well enough to undertake
the class for the women prisoners, this experience started her on
her state, national, and international crusade for intelligent and
adequate provision for the insane.

Starting out on the theory that if the things which she had seen
were possible in an East Cambridge jail, they might be found in other
jails or almshouses of Massachusetts, for two years Miss Dix visited,
notebook in hand, the jails and almshouses in every county in the

state. She next presented her findings in a remarkable memorial to the Legislature of Massachusetts, in which she described how the insane were then "confined within that Commonwealth, in cages, closets, cellars, stalls, pens; chained, naked, beaten with rods and lashed into obedience." How annually with the town's poor, they were put up at auction and given to the care of the lowest bidders: ignorant men who fed them through the iron bars of their cages, threw water over them from time to time; left them often exposed to the public view, hungry, naked and filthy, their ravings a subject of mirth.

Miss Dix's memorial was, however, much more than a recital of human interest stories of the sort that would have satisfied the most impatient of our present-day newspaper friends. She submitted to the legislature a plan for a change in the whole system. Intelligent and adequate care through the local poor officials was clearly impossible; she urged immediate enlargement of the State facilities so as to provide modern care by the State of all the poor insane. The opposition which she met in Massachusetts was typical of that she met everywhere. Local keepers who made a miserable livelihood out of the local care of these unfortunates, their friends, and the local merchants who derived a little or perhaps a large profit by furnishing supplies to the jails and almshouses, assailed her facts and her motives. They urged the necessity of reducing taxes and the importance of local responsibility in our whole scheme of government. But investigation only substantiated her statements and her first bill providing for the enlargement of the Worcester Hospital passed the Legislature.

Deciding that, if these conditions could exist in Massachusetts, they could exist in other States, Dorothea Dix started on her national campaign. What she had done in Massachusetts was repeated in every State. North and south, east and west, she visited jails and almshouses, traveling by train, by boat, on horseback, by stage coach, and prairie schooner. Everywhere she found only local variations of the hideous brutality she had found in Massachusetts; everywhere she met the same type of opposition. The importance of local initiative and the dangers of state consolidation was in every state the principle behind which inhuman treatment of the insane sought to hide. In state after state she triumphed by reliance upon the theory that, if the facts are known, relief will be forthcoming.

This was a time when the great public domain of the Middle West was being given to individual homesteaders, to railroads to encourage the building of the transcontinental lines and to the states as a permanent educational foundation. With evidence of a national need, Miss Dix asked that Congress set aside first 5,000,000 and later 12,225,000 acres of land as a national endowment for the care of the insane. She presented her first memorial to Congress in 1848; in 1854 this bill actually passed only to be vetoed by President Pierce. This was only twelve years after the first chance visit to the county jail in East Cambridge. The story of those twelve incredibly strenuous years leaves one both depressed and comforted.

Miss Dix's biographer thus describes her legislative methods: ". . . So profound was the impression made by her exceptional personality that an especial room was habitually set aside for her, in which to be visited by the members. There she studied the list of the representatives, endeavoring to find out the character of each for humanity or self-seeking, courage or servility to public opinion. She did not, however, herself enter the halls of legislation, nor seek interviews of the members in their homes or in the lobbies. Always she laid great stress on preserving her womanly dignity, and saw plainly how easy it was to vulgarize alike a cause and its representative by a pushing and teasing demeanor. Members of either house were brought in by influential friends to her own room or alcove, and there she wrought on them in every way of cogent argument and eloquent entreaty. The only exception to this, of a slightly more public nature, was her habit of inviting into the parlor of her boarding-house from fifteen to twenty gentlemen at a time, for conversation and discussion."

This was her method in the states. In Washington a special alcove in the Capitol Library, now separately housed and no longer useful for such purposes, is said to have been set apart for her use and here she was visited by Senators and Congressmen. Apparently legislators of the 1840s were not altogether unlike those of the 1920s.

Miss Dix writes that it was not the blunt country member whom she feared, but the one who referred to her as a "Heaven sent angel of mercy." For example, one Senator who began "None, sir, is a firmer friend than myself to this charity . . ." and continued, "But, sir, my experience, limited as it is, has taught me that the same law governs in the moral as in the physical world, and that premature development is attended by premature decay. . . . It becomes us, therefore, to be borne away by no childlike sensibility, no generous enthusiasm, no over-zeal nor haste to accomplish an acknowledged good. . . . Under these views and feelings, therefore, I am constrained, Mr. President, at this time, to oppose this project under every aspect it may now assume before us. . . .

"In conclusion, I should do injustice to my feelings if I omitted this occasion to express my unlimited admiration of the distinguished zeal and ability with which this measure has been prosecuted by the remarkable lady who, it is but due to her to say, has been its chief promoter and friend. . . . Woman, Mr. President, is ever lovely, and when she assumes the rare and sacred office of disinterested philanthropy she becomes indeed an angel!"

To many women this has a strangely familiar sound. I remember in the suffrage debates in Congress how almost every man rose to explain the reasons why women were not wise or foolish enough to be trusted with the ballot, referred to his "sainted mother" or described the perilous height of the pedestal on which he placed his wife and all women.

President Pierce's veto of the land bill had arguments not unfamiliar. Explaining that he had "been compelled to resist the deep sympathies of his own heart in favor of the humane purposes sought to be accomplished" by the bill, he made it clear that while recognizing the right of Congress to grant lands on a lavish scale for schools, colleges, railroads, and other internal improvement, he was sure the foundations of the republic would be undermined if there were any national aid for the insane. "The fountains of charity," he declared, "will be dried up at home, and the several States, instead of bestowing their own means on the social wants of their own people, may themselves become humble suppliants for the bounty of the Federal government, reversing their true relation to this Union." Words which have a familiar sound.

After this defeat, Dorothea Dix's efforts on behalf of the insane did not end, but it is not possible to chronicle her work in other countries here. For our purposes the especially significant facts are her method of work.

She began always with careful assembling of the facts as to existing conditions, secured information as to the then best method of treatment, and on this basis of fact and possibility she was satisfied with nothing less than a revolution in the system that then prevailed.

Her interest included the insane in every place and she traversed every avenue where help could be found.

Today we are not individual crusaders. National organizations, especially ones like the General Federation of Women's Clubs with its 4,000,000 members scattered throughout the country, seek to use [their] membership for promoting public welfare. Our first step today as in Dorothea Dix's time is investigation—a knowledge of the facts. The objectives, the standards which are to serve as a measuring rod in evaluating facts must also be determined. . . .

Having agreed upon our objective, our standards, the next step is to have exact information. . . . The membership of the organization which urges the legislation should understand the reason why the legislation is sought and what will be accomplished. Endorsement without understanding is and should be of little value.

. . . Finally, the measure must be guided through the legislature. While the legislative committee or agent needs to know legislative rules and procedures and be aware of the pitfalls that beset the path of any bill, no measure, and especially a social welfare measure, should be passed by tricks or skillful eleventh-hour maneuvering. We should see to it that it is not defeated by such tactics, but the legislative campaign should be from the beginning to the end an educational one.

Suppose all these requisites have been fulfilled and the women who represent women's organizations appear before Congressional and legislative committees. Will they encounter any special difficulties because they are women and the measures which they advocate are the special concern of women? With few exceptions the value of the laws they recommend cannot be adequately measured by the usual business standards by which men have been trained to evaluate results. . . . Do we need to resort to so inadequate a measure of values? . . .

Women's methods have always been cautious but determined. They are that in politics. They expect to "conquer because their cause is just" rather than because they are to be feared on election day. It is this, together with their faith in democracy, that sustains them in the face of defeat. This, in itself, is something of a contribution to political life. But to some it may seem to be the measure of their political inexperience.

The American nation is supposed to combine idealism with practical common sense as does no other nation. Two things are certain. Women have no intention of abandoning either their idealism or their belief in the practical value of political persistence. Their responsibility to children makes either impossible.

Members of State Legislatures and of Congress need the same information on which you reach your conclusions—a knowledge of the facts to be corrected, the methods which you propose, the support which you have for your proposal, and whether it is an experiment or has the weight of experience behind it. For this reason, the importance of an educated and interested club membership cannot be overestimated. You owe it to your legislative committee, to the club, to the legislators, to the entire community to know what you are standing for and why you are standing for it. You have a right to undertake a course in compulsory education of public officials in community needs, but you must first be able to pass a teacher's examination. The community looks to women for expert opinions on certain groups of subjects. We become experts not because of intuitive understanding of these subjects but because we devote our time and our intelligence to understanding them. Legislative technique is the technique of adult education. It should be based on absolute honesty of purpose, a fearless facing of the facts and a devotion in the face of opposition and ridicule to the ends which we know to be right.

SEVENTEEN

Women

Review of *Angels and Amazons*
by Inez Haynes Irwin, 1933[1]

They are, of course, neither angels nor amazons. These women of whom Inez Haynes Irwin writes had a little more courage, some more ability or a greater concern over injustices than, shall we say, the median woman. That their story has been given this alliterative title suggests to me the anomaly of what was called the Lecture Room at Hull House. I remember an Italian girl explained to me when I was a new resident at the House, "Lectures not there. No. Dances often. Maybe that's why it's called Lecture Hall." Had these women been angels or amazons, the book would have had fewer readers and much less comment from reviewers. For women . . . are news. The man of the street has a theory as to what their role should be. College professors, ministers, husbands, and women themselves also know. A college president announces that the employment of women outside their own homes is the cause of our present unemployment. His theory has no factual basis, but something is certainly wrong; let women return to their homes and firesides. It would only increase his impatience to ask if they will have homes and firesides if they do not work. Perhaps the women he knows do have.

A biologist announces that women are mentally, morally, and physically inferior to men. It is front-page news. Some men find it accords with their own experience, and some women accept it as an explanation of their own failures. A psychologist tells us that women who have proven their capacity in literature, in science, in art, in the professions, or in social services are not happy. They may imagine that they are, but he knows that they cannot be. Their lives are in conflict with their subconscious selves. It is not in point, of course, to ask are men as happy now as their grandfathers were. They at least are not at war with their destiny as modern women are said to be. Moreover, someone is sure to suggest that the explanation of unhappy man is unhappy woman.

Mrs. Irwin does not ask or answer such questions as these. She tells, with pride in their accomplishments, the story of the American women who were the first to undertake some activity new to their sex, or who have helped to open doors that were closed to most women a century ago. She is sure that there have been great gains for women in the tremendous changes of the past hundred years. . . . Mrs. Irwin set out, she tells us, to tell the story of woman's progress "as manifested and evidenced through their organizations." But she has not held rigidly to this plan and she does not give us the fresh and interesting material about women's clubs which Prof. Breckinridge has assembled in her Social Trends monograph— "Women in the Twentieth Century"—which was also published this summer.[2] Mrs. Irwin finds the individual woman more interesting than the organization of which she may be a member. . . .

However, . . . Mrs. Irwin succeeds in communicating to the reader her excitement and enthusiasm over the victories which have been achieved by women during the past century and the book should help to promote what she hopes will be further gains during the next century.

EIGHTEEN

The Changing Position of
Women in Government

Address given for the National Women's Republican Clubs, 1930

It is approximately ten years since the Nineteenth Amendment was ratified, and this is perhaps why my subject has been included at this 1930 Annual Meeting of the National Women's Republican Clubs.

Some of you may think that I have been more than usually foolish to accept the invitation to discuss it because, being *in* and *of* the Government, any expressions of discontent with the progress made might be taken to have a personal bearing. But to me such a conclusion seems fantastic. Although not so rated on social lists of the State Department or so regarded by our friends, the press, no one in the National Government has a more important function than the promotion of the welfare of the children of the United States. I have no official interest in the position of women in Government—or, more accurately, in the attitude of men in places of influence toward women in Government—except as it affects the performance of my duties as Chief of the Children's Bureau.

While that is my official interest in the subject, my personal interest as a citizen and as a woman is as wide and as deep as the subject itself.

I take it that you are especially interested, to use an expression now current in Washington, in what the application of a yard stick to the progress of women in Government now as compared with ten, twenty, or fifty years ago [shows].

Her biographer tells us that Clara Barton was the first woman clerk to be employed by the Federal Government some seventy-five years ago. I am not sure that it is true, but I hope it is. In a sense, this great achievement may be said to detract from the later triumphs of Miss Barton which are so much more widely known. It is not surprising that, having succeeded in her determination to use pen and ink as a copy clerk in the service of the Government, she had no hesitancy in asking for passes to the front line for herself and her kit of jellies and bandages and medicines.

"I shall give battle front service," she said, when she arranged for her clerical tasks to be performed by her fellow clerks who remained in Washington. To some of us, it seems as though she must have given "battle front service" when in the 1850s she succeeded in breaking down the prejudice which had up to that time prevented any woman from entering the Government service.

As you know, forced by the exigencies of the Civil War, the numbers of women in the Government service increased greatly during the 1860s, just as they did during the World War. I am sure this admission of women to the lowest ranks of officialdom was regarded by many men, particularly those who spoke in the most exalted terms of the "sacred calling of women," as one of the horrors that the Civil War brought.

The progress of women in government from 1860 to the present was not rapid. In the analysis made . . . for the Women's Bureau of the civil service examinations that were open and those that were not open to women during a six months' period in 1919, women were excluded from 60 percent of all examinations held, from 64 percent of the examinations for scientific and professional positions, and from 87 percent in the mechanical and manufacturing services. This report was submitted to the Civil Service Commission and, ten days after receiving the report, the Commission passed a ruling opening all examinations to both women and men, which left women free to compete in the examinations and the appointing officers free to appoint men, if they preferred men. What the preference of the appointing officers was, the Women's Bureau discovered six years later in a second survey. It showed that only 16 percent of the women—as compared with 51.8 precent of the men—received salaries of $1,860 or more per annum. . . .

A recent editorial in the *New York Times* commented on the fact that the director of the census was appointing twenty-four women as supervisors . . . [in 1930], when only five women were so honored in 1920. No mention was made of the fact that this was 24 out of 546 already appointed, and out of a total of 574 supervisors to be appointed.

The closing sentences of the editorial were as follows: "In addition to this valuable work, there will be many jobs of less prominence for women. They will do much of the house-to-house canvassing, and a large share of the clerical work will fall to them." That, I think, describes the situation in most Government bureaus.

The story of women in major executive positions is a very short one. Miss Lathrop was appointed Chief of the Children's Bureau in 1912 by President Taft and a woman was continued in this position when she resigned. Between 1917 and 1920, when there was a lively expectation of immediate political power for women, women were first appointed by President Wilson to the following positions: Chief of the Women's Bureau, member of the Civil Service Commission, assistant attorney general (which carried the status of an assistant secretary), and commissioner for the District of Columbia. Secretaries and bureau chiefs also opened the doors to a number of less important offices carrying administrative responsibility during that period.

Women were reappointed to all of these positions when the Republicans returned to power in 1920, except that of District Commissioner. Additional first appointments were made then. A woman was appointed for the first time as chairman of the Federal Employers Compensation Commission; the House Economics Bureau was created in the Department of Agriculture, and a woman under civil service appointment was promoted by the secretary to be director of the Bureau; women were admitted for the first time to the diplomatic service and a few minor appointments of women to this service were made; two or three women were made assistant trade commissioners in the Bureau of Foreign and Interstate Commerce; women were appointed to serve as collectors of Internal Revenue for the first time; and a few were appointed by bureau chiefs to minor executive positions in the scientific services, which had never been held by women before. . . .

If we try to evaluate the present position of women in the executive branch, not by the total numbers employed, but by the number holding important positions, we must, I think, say that women, up to this time, have had little or no recognition in the administrative branch of our Federal Government.

There are more women in Congress than in 1921—one then, as compared with eight today. Although still only a little band, this increase is encouraging and, I think it is safe to say that the members can do their work more easily now than the same women could ten years ago. The Senate still awaits the coming of a woman—but it would not use the word "await" in the sense that you or I would on this subject.

In the judicial branch no appointment of a woman has yet been made, so there we are exactly where we were in 1920—nothing equals nothing.

In view of the ten years that have lapsed since the nineteenth amendment was adopted it may seem to the impatient observer an evidence that women are, in fact, losing rather than gaining ground. Patience is not a virtue of mine, but I know we must take a long view on this question of women in Government. We need to examine ourselves and the environment in which we must work from a factual standpoint.

The most frequently asked question is, who or what is responsible for our failure to gain more ground? Is it because the Republican party has not given us a chance to carry the ball? Well, it is the party in power. But as I am about to reach a conclusion, I think also of the strong and wholly articulate opposition party. I have read and listened to many statements by Democrats about what the Republican party and the Republican President have done or left undone, but I have never heard a whisper of or read a word of masculine democratic criticism about what the Republican party or the Republican President might have done for women. I think the Democratic women could tell you why.

I come from the middle-west—the western middle-west—where the contributions of the pioneer women are a matter of memory and of frequent reference by many people. It is the region from which the progressive Republican bloc in Congress comes. But even they, so far as I know, have not pointed out the injustice, the wastefulness of the present failure to utilize the contributions which women might make in our Government.

The modern political Diogenes, we are told, is going about with a lantern in his hand seeking not an honest man, but the perfect woman to appoint to office. She must, of course, be lovely, well-dressed, but not a leader of fashion; able, yet in the habit of constantly concealing that fact. She must have had much political experience so that the politician will say, "she deserved the job." On the other hand, she must bring such technical training and technical experience to the position that the newspapers and the independent voter will say, "This was not a political appointment, but evidence of a policy of selecting only those of special qualification for the work." It is easy to predict that such women will not often be found.

A cynic has suggested to me that if women did not have the vote, the easy answer to all our difficulties would be our old slogan, "Votes for women." Yes, that would be the answer just as, if farmers did not have the right to vote, we could solve at once this problem of farm relief by votes for farmers.

"Votes for women" supplies the general ticket of admission to the political fairgrounds, but not to the side shows. But general admission *is* general admission, and, in spite of all that might be said that is depressing about women in government, our position might be worse.

I am much under the spell of Virginia Woolf's very clever book, *A Room of One's Own*. You have, I am sure, been reading it, and I hope you will not object to my quoting from it some this afternoon. Mrs. Woolf was discussing women as novelists and poets, but what she has said applies equally well to women in government, or in business, or in the professions—to any effort of women toward freedom in the effective expression of her convictions and the utilization of her capacities. You remember she points out how unpleasant it is to be locked out, but how much worse to be locked in. We are no longer locked in our homes, and we are not locked in the citadel of a political party—and by that token we are still free to negotiate the terms on which we shall be admitted—what we will surrender for what we are to receive.

I hope no one will suppose that I am discouraged at the progress that women have made. At least not when I think about it in the morning, although I confess I often take real discouragement to bed with me at night. We must remember that the woman voter, in most parts of the United States of America, has only a decade of experience, and her position in government depends upon the value at which her political experience is assessed. This description of a young woman novelist undertaking to tell her story in what seems to her the best way applies equally well to the woman voter in 1920:

"At any rate, she was making an attempt. And as I watched her lengthening out for the test, I saw, but hoped that she did not see, the bishops and the deans, the doctors and the professors, the patriarchs and the pedagogues all at her shouting warning and advice. You can't do this and you shan't do that: Fellows and scholars only allowed on the grass! Ladies not admitted without a letter of introduction! Aspiring and graceful female novelists this way! So they kept at her like the crowd at a fence on the race-course, and it was her trial to take her fence without looking to right or left. If you stop to curse you are lost, I said to her; equally, if you stop to laugh. Hesitate or fumble and you are done for. Think only of the jump, I implored her, as if I had put the whole of my money on her back; and she went over it like a bird. But there was a fence beyond that and a fence beyond that. Whether she had the staying power, I was doubtful, for the clapping and the crying were fraying to the nerves."

Well, your presence here today is proof that no man should hastily decide that women lack the staying quality. On the contrary, one of the common criticisms is that we are too logical and too persistent— we do not know when to compromise and what of our principles to forget. You know these qualities were formerly considered virtues in men, but, having been discovered to be more frequently present in women, the viewpoint is changed. What should be regarded as assets are counted as liabilities.

May I illustrate? We have recently learned a good deal about the correction of speech defect, of which the most common is stammering. The treatment has brought out some statistics as to the number and the sex of stammerers. I was surprised to find that in one place, the boy stammerers outnumbered the girls in the ratio of sixteen to one, and in another place as ten to one. Here at last, I said to myself, the girls have an advantage. They can make a forthright statement more easily than boys. But an English professor learnedly sets out the theory that this is boldness. This lack of diffidence in women, which reduces stuttering among us, only proves—the professor is sure—that women are less civilized than men.

The difficulty is, of course, to accept differences without a conclusion as to superiority.

§

"Life at best," Mrs. Woolf reminds us, "is arduous, difficult, a perpetual struggle. It calls for gigantic courage and strength. More than anything, perhaps, creatures of illusion as we are, it calls for confidence in oneself. Without self-confidence we are as babes in the cradle." Self-confidence is of slow growth. In his book entitled *Understanding Human Nature,* Alfred Adler says, "It is a frequently overlooked fact that a girl comes into the world with a prejudice sounding in her ears which is designed to rob her of her belief in her value, to shatter her self-confidence and destroy her hope of ever doing anything worth while." Less than in the past, and less in the United States than in other countries, this sense of inferiority on the part of girls and of superiority on the part of boys is being deliberately cultivated.

Some women and some men wonder why change in the position of woman has been desired. Repeatedly they ask, "Why should anyone choose the 'strenuous life'? seek a part in the struggle to end the injustice and ugliness of our modern life?" They are the lotus-eaters, who prefer to live in a gray twilight in which there is neither victory nor defeat. It is impossible for them to understand: that to have had a part in the struggle—to have done what one could—is in itself the reward of effort and the comfort in defeat.

Perhaps the greatest achievements of the Children's Bureau were the policies carried on so ably by Grace Abbott, which made the women throughout the country realize that the Bureau belonged to them and that the government was functioning not only on their behalf, but through their own participation.

The Children's Bureau not only has rendered a great humanitarian and scientific service to the children of the nation, but has actually worked out methods for endearing the federal government to millions of its citizens. To unite a great source of human energy like maternal affection with governmental functions was no small contribution to the art of government which is so slowly being evolved throughout the centuries.

—JANE ADDAMS, winner of the Nobel Peace Prize

Postscript

Dr. Jeanne C. Marsh
Dean of the School of Social Service Administration,
University of Chicago

From the beginning, Grace and Edith Abbott knew that others would
need to be engaged in "the struggle." And from their earliest days
of working and living at Hull House, they started to create training programs that would teach others to do what they themselves
were learning to do: analyze and address the most important social
problems of our society. The Abbott sisters' work among immigrants—especially the women and children of that world-renowned
Chicago settlement house—contributed greatly to the development
of professional social work in America.

As the dean of the very school of social service that Edith Abbott
helped to found (the School of Civics and Philanthropy, now the
University of Chicago's School of Social Service Administration,
or SSA), I am particularly intrigued by the way the writings in this
collection attest to the most salient issues of our own day, and to
the values that form the bedrock of the social work profession today. They describe the importance of gathering information "first
hand" from those in need of assistance, and of documenting and
analyzing problems locally as well as nationally.

Both Abbott sisters had a profound confidence in these early social
welfare research efforts. Grace believed so strongly in the power
of facts that she felt they could even "transcend political theory or
political traditions." And Edith devoted her career to building a
graduate program of social work education that set the standard

for all programs that have followed. The Abbotts struggled against the "ignorance and indifference . . . of social policies that . . . failed to consider the complex character of our population."

The Abbott sisters, with their mutual concerns and from their respective platforms, shared resources, ideas, and ideals. If, for instance, an SSA student came up with a particularly incisive research question, Dean Abbott in Chicago would often make the question known to Chief Abbott in Washington DC—for the Children's Bureau might be able to support the study and then put the findings to work shaping national policy. Similarly, if a serious problem at the Children's Bureau arose, Grace Abbott might seek out, via her sister Edith at SSA, the best researchers to track down its cause.

Their struggles back then remain our struggles today. As SSA celebrates the one-hundredth anniversary of its founding in 1908, one thing I have most appreciated in this fascinating and useful book is the pervasive belief that the success of any endeavor depends on the quality of the people undertaking the work. To do good social work, we need good social workers—women and men who are able, committed, well trained, and respected by their society.

The Abbott sisters were extraordinary exemplars of the qualities needed to do good social work. This volume is a reminder of what we in America have achieved, and the great distance we have yet to go.

Source Acknowledgments

"Hull House Days," by Edith Abbott, excerpted from "A Sister's Memories," unpublished manuscript, Grace Abbott Papers, Edith Abbott Memorial Library, Grand Island NE.

"The Immigrant Girl," by Grace Abbott, from "Within the City's Gates," *Chicago Evening Post*, December 23, 1909.

"The Education of Foreigners in American Citizenship," by Grace Abbott, Report of the School Extension Committee, printed in the *Proceedings of the of the Buffalo Conference for Good City Government and the Sixteenth Annual Meeting of the National Municipal League*, ed. Clinton Rogers Woodruff (Buffalo: National Municipal League, 1910), 375–84.

"The Immigrant as a Problem in Community Planning," by Grace Abbott, *Publications of the American Sociological Society* 12 (1916): 166–73.

"Problems of the Immigrant Girl," by Grace Abbott, in *The Immigrant and the Community*, by Grace Abbott (New York: The Century Company, 1917).

"The Maternity and Infancy Revolution," by Edith Abbott, excerpted from "A Sister's Memories," unpublished manuscript, Grace Abbott Papers, Edith Abbott Memorial Library, Grand Island NE, and printed in *Maternal and Child Health Journal* 8, no. 3 (2004): 107–10.

"A Constitutional Amendment," by Grace Abbott, in *Collier's*, November 17, 1920.

"Public Protection for Children," by Grace Abbott, speech given at the National Conference of Social Work, Toronto, June 1924, Grace Abbott Papers, Edith Abbott Memorial Library, Grand Island NE, and printed in *Proceedings of the National Conference of Social Work* (Chicago: University of Chicago Press for the National Conference of Social Work, 1924), 3–14.

"Perpetuating May Day," by Grace Abbott, *New York Herald Tribune*, May 5, 1929.

"The Next Steps," by Grace Abbott, speech given at the Twenty-Fifth Anniversary Conference of the National Child Labor Committee, New York City, December 16–17, 1929, Grace Abbott Papers, Edith Abbott Memorial Library, Grand Island NE.

"Boarding Out," Grace Abbott, a speech given for Maurice Bisgeyer of the National Association of Jewish Centers, Washington DC, November 6, 1930, Grace Abbott Papers, Edith Abbott Memorial Library, Grand Island NE.

"The Challenge of Child Welfare," by Grace Abbott, speech given at the Annual Convention of the American National Red Cross, Washington DC, April 14, 1931, Grace Abbott Papers, Edith Abbott Memorial Library, Grand Island NE.

"The Real American Vice," by Grace Abbott, presented at the Conference of State and Provincial Health Authorities of North America, April 29, 1931, Grace Abbott Papers, Edith Abbott Memorial Library, Grand Island NE.

"The Washington Traffic Jam," by Grace Abbott, acceptance speech given for her Gold Medal from the National Institute of Social Sciences, May 7, 1931, Grace Abbott Papers, Edith Abbott Memorial Library, Grand Island NE.

"Why Did Child Labor Ever Develop in America?" by Grace Abbott, unpublished paper, University of Chicago, ca. 1933, Grace Abbott Papers, Edith Abbott Memorial Library, Grand Island NE.

"Promoting the Welfare of All Children," by Grace Abbott, speech given at the Children's Bureau Dinner, Washington DC, April 8, 1937, Grace Abbott Papers, Edith Abbott Memorial Library, Grand Island NE.

"Children and the Depression," by Grace Abbott, in *From Relief to Social Security* (Chicago: University of Chicago Press, 1941). Reprinted by permission of the University of Chicago Press.

"How Women Achieve in Government," by Frances Perkins, *The Child* (August 1939).

"Dorothea Dix," by Grace Abbott, speech given at the biennial convention for the General Federation of Women's Clubs, Atlantic City NJ, May 27, 1926, Grace Abbott Papers, Edith Abbott Memorial Library, Grand Island NE.

"Women," by Grace Abbott, review of *Angels and Amazons* by Inez Haynes Irwin, 1933, Grace Abbott Papers, Edith Abbott Memorial Library, Grand Island NE.

"The Changing Position of Women in Government," by Grace Abbott, speech given to the National Women's Republican Clubs, 1930.

Notes

Hull House Days

1. Edith Abbott first published excerpts from this memoir of her sister Grace's life in the September 1939 issue of *Social Service Review*. She continued working on the never-completed full-length manuscript until shortly before her own death in 1957. A relatively inclusive draft was completed in 1952, around the time of Edith Abbott's retirement from the School of Social Service Administration in Chicago and her return to Grand Island, Nebraska.

2. Formed in 1907, the Immigrants' Protective League emerged from a committee established by the Women's Trade Union League to investigate working conditions faced by young female immigrants. Grace Abbott served as its first director.

1. The Immigrant Girl

1. From 1909 to 1910 Grace Abbott wrote a series of weekly articles about immigrants for the *Chicago Evening Post*.

2. The Education of Foreigners in American Citizenship

1. Jane Addams (1860–1935) was a prominent American social reformer and peace activist. Cofounder of the famous Chicago settlement house, Hull House, Addams received the Nobel Peace Prize in 1931.

2. The Naturalization Act of 1795 made a five-year period of residence a requirement of all foreign-born individuals seeking American citizenship. Despite numerous efforts to lengthen the time, the requirement remained the legal benchmark, later supplemented by written examinations focused on basic knowledge of the American Constitution. However in the early twentieth century, other legislation illustrated a growing hostility to

newcomers. In 1917 Congress authorized a literacy test for immigrants, over President Woodrow Wilson's veto, and legislation in 1924 established strict immigration quotas, skewed to prefer those of northern European background.

3. The Immigrant as a Problem in Community Planning

1. In 1911 Grace Abbott received three month's leave from her position with the Immigrants' Protective League and traveled to Europe to visit the countries from which most of the "new" immigrants came to Chicago. Abbott spent most of her time in the Austro-Hungarian empire visiting remote villages of the rural countryside.

2. In the forty years between 1870 and 1910, more than twenty-five million immigrants came to the United States. This huge influx of newcomers was unprecedented, spurred by transportation revolutions that made sea travel cheaper and much quicker. While still primarily of European origins, the turn-of-the-century "new" immigrants were different from the Irish and Germans who preceded them. They shared neither the English language nor Protestant faith with native-born Americans. They were Jews, Catholics, and Eastern Orthodox, overwhelmingly hailing from southern and eastern Europe rather than from northern Europe, as had previously been the case.

The Maternity and Infancy Revolution

1. Julia Lathrop (1858–1952) was an American social reformer, a settlement house advocate, and an early colleague of Jane Addams. Lathrop helped found the Immigrants' Protective League and served as the first head of the U.S. Children's Bureau from 1912 to 1921.

2. The Sheppard-Towner Maternity and Infancy Act, cosponsored by Senator Morris Sheppard (D-Texas) and Representative Horace Towner (R-Iowa) and signed into law in 1921, was the first joint federal-state cost-sharing program to encourage better prenatal and infant care in the United States. The Children's Bureau administered the program from 1921 to 1929, when Congress failed to renew enabling legislation.

3. Sheppard-Towner funds supported the establishment of almost three thousand "well baby" and prenatal diagnostic health centers.

4. Grace Abbott herself took a certain satisfaction in her position as Chief of the Children's Bureau, as may be noted in her comment to the press, "If I am an ambassador, I feel that, judged by the numbers I represent, the rank of the Ambassador of Children of the U.S. should be very high" (Edith and Grace Abbott Papers, University of Chicago Library).

5. A Constitutional Amendment

1. *Collier's* was a mass-circulation journal published from 1888 to 1957 that was known for its reform agenda and that campaigned for woman suffrage and against child labor. The magazine was the first to publish excerpts from Upton Sinclair's famous exposé of the meat-packing industry, *The Jungle.*

2. Grace Abbott refers here to a famous essay, written by the nation's first Secretary of the Treasury, Alexander Hamilton, that urged utilizing the labor of women and children in still-infant American industries in order to spare men for farming and westward expansion.

3. See the introduction to this volume for further discussion on the Child Labor Tax Act.

4. The Children's Amendment was passed by Congress and sent to the states in 1924. The proposed Twentieth Amendment to the U.S. Constitution gave Congress the power to limit, regulate, and prohibit the labor of all persons under the age of eighteen. At a time when labor codes in many states counted only those under age fifteen as children, the so-called Child Labor Amendment was far ahead of most official understandings of child labor. The passage of the Nineteenth Amendment (woman suffrage) in 1920 convinced a sufficient number of U.S. Congressmen that women wanted far more dramatic federal regulation in support of young workers. Grace Abbott certainly did, but the amendment never won sufficient national support to be ratified.

6. Public Protection for Children

1. By the 1930s the National Conference of Social Work (NCSW) was the primary organizational vehicle for promoting discussion between social workers from around the nation. Its proceedings remain a primary source for students of the history of social work in the United States.

2. Great increases in support for public education occurred between 1905 and 1925, though "inevitable" probably expressed Grace Abbott's typical optimism.

3. Until the nineteenth century this concept of "parish responsibility" was the centuries-old principle upon which poor relief rested.

4. Grace Abbott was an enthusiastic supporter of such "state centralization"—especially at the federal level. Her advocacy met a great deal more concerted opposition than the first part of this sentence indicates.

5. Dorothea Dix (1802–1887) was an American social reformer notable for her advocacy of better treatment for the mentally ill.

6. The world to which Grace Abbott refers primarily centered in Europe

and the British Commonwealth countries of Australia, New Zealand, and Canada, though she does not make this distinction clear. In the late 1930s in a booklet for the League of Nations Grace Abbott wrote, "Child welfare has no national boundaries. The needs of underfed, neglected, and delinquent children do not differ widely from nation to nation. The future of the world will be affected by the way in which such children are cared for now. Large groups of disadvantaged children are a menace, not only to the future of the countries in which they live, but to the peace of the world" (Edith and Grace Abbott Papers, University of Chicago Library).

7. Grace Abbott may have been referring here to the Smith-Lever Act of 1914 and the Smith-Hughes Act of 1917, both of which provided federal support for vocational education. Both bills emphasized teaching "general" or practical job skills to adults as well as children. Beyond this, federal aid to education was quite limited in 1924 and remained limited for decades to come. The U.S. Congress only authorized a federal Department of Education as recently as 1979, though a much smaller Office of Education had been a tiny branch within the Department of the Interior since the mid-nineteenth century.

8. Mary Richmond (1861–1928) was a pioneering social work educator and prolific author. Richmond was the longtime head of the Russell Sage Foundation's Charity Organization Department and a founder of the New York School of Social Work, later known as Columbia University's School of Social Work.

9. A statement related to this talk was made by Grace Abbott in a speech that she gave to the National Education Association in Philadelphia, Pennsylvania, on June 28, 1926: "We sometimes forget that provisions for education, for health, for recreation, are made possible for all children only through law. We sometimes forget, too, that while all children are not in need of these agencies that the public purse makes available, some of the children need all of them, and all of the children need some of them. There is no parent, however wise and rich and resourceful, that can successfully rear his children without the cooperation of the community" (Edith and Grace Abbott Papers, University of Chicago Library).

7. Perpetuating May Day
1. It is possible that in the title of this article Grace Abbott plays on some of the more radical images associated with May 1, or "May Day."

2. The National Child Health Day tradition preceded President Hoover's administration. It began during World War I, though the name varied slightly over the years.

3. Organized in 1923 the American Child Health Association consolidated the American Child Hygiene Association and the Child Health Organization. Secretary of Commerce Herbert Hoover served as its president.

4. In 1918 two identical but separately submitted bills initiated a Congressional process that eventually led to the passage of the Sheppard-Towner Maternity and Infancy Act of 1921. Representative Jeannette Rankin (R-Montana) and Senator Joseph Robinson (D-Arkansas) introduced bills that called for the federal government to appropriate money to encourage "instruction in the hygiene of maternity of infancy"—contingent on states' appropriating matching funds. Both bills died in committee.

5. The nature of birth records was still very incomplete in the early twentieth century. Grace Abbott may have believed this statistic to be accurate, but it was likely a rough estimate.

6. See note 2 in "The Maternity and Infancy Revolution" in this volume.

7. Concerning the mortality of mothers in childbirth, Grace Abbott also wrote, "Pregnancy is not a disease. Lowering the death rate of women in childbirth to an irreducible minimum is necessary for the social and economic security of the home" ("Toward Security in Health," *The Survey* [February 1935]).

8. The Next Steps

1. Organized in 1904 the National Child Labor Committee carried on a nationwide investigation of children's employment and campaigned for stronger legislation and better enforcement.

2. See the introduction in this volume for a discussion of early federal child labor law.

3. Grace and Edith Abbott contributed important scholarship on delinquency and played a role in popularizing the term beyond academic circles.

4. In January 1909 President Theodore Roosevelt hosted the first White House Conference on Dependent Children. One of the meeting's most important recommendations urged the creation of a federal-level children's bureau.

5. After the passage of the restrictive 1924 National Origins Act, the percentage of immigrants in the total national population dropped from an average of 15 percent in the years from 1900 to 1920 to under 6 percent until the Immigration Act of 1965 redefined and liberalized U.S. immigration policy.

6. Dr. Alfred Adler was a Viennese psychologist who argued that per-

sonality could be best explained by the human need to surmount innate feelings of inferiority. Adler established child guidance centers in Europe that were used as models by his American disciples.

7. Grace Abbott regularly spoke about the workers and methods needed in the struggle for children's rights. She addressed these issues in terms that were both inspirational and pragmatic. In a talk to the National Women's Trade Union League, for instance, she pointed out, "It is a relatively few people who do accomplish things that must be done. It is a few who really care and keep steadily on the job, who finally convert the larger groups." And in a newspaper interview she added, "If we are going to get money voted to us that is adequate to meet our need, we have to let the [public] know what we are doing, why we are doing it, and what the needs really are, because they won't know any other way. . . . You can't disregard public opinion. In your small town, you have to try to carry the [public] along with you, and not just give them up as hopeless. They are reasonable people. The bulk of them are as reasonable as the rest of us. At any rate, you can't just disregard them" (Edith and Grace Abbott Papers, University of Chicago Library).

9. Boarding Out

1. The acceptance of this idea (ca. 1930) was still relatively new. An earlier generation of social and charity workers had embraced the orphanage.

2. Between 1911 and 1930 forty-six of the existing forty-eight states enacted "mothers' pensions," providing public assistance to impoverished "worthy" mothers to enable them to raise young children at home. Most states defined worthiness narrowly, granting aid only to white widows. Moreover, most provided very limited funds even to this group. The onset of the Great Depression ended most pension initiatives, though Social Security's Title IV "Aid to Dependent Children" program revived and federalized them in 1935.

Regarding government responsibility for children, Grace Abbott also wrote, "If there is any subject endowed with national interest it is the welfare of the nation's children. The nation's future existence, the intelligent use of its resources, the role it will play in world affairs, depend on its children—on whether they are physically fit, have been trained in self-control, in respect for the rights of others, and in understanding of their own rights and obligations. The first responsibility for the child rests upon the parent. But there are services which the government, the municipality, the county, and the state must supply to aid the parents and to assume responsibility when the parental care fails. The federal government, through the Children's Bureau, plays the role of an interested and, we hope, intelligent cooperator, ready to assist but not to control nor hamper" ("Children's Bureau," *Childhood Education* 5 [March 1929]).

10. The Challenge of Child Welfare

1. Throughout the Depression years Grace Abbott drew attention (often much to the irritation of President Hoover) to the relationship between employment and child welfare. Only a few weeks before giving this speech she wrote, "Perhaps the most important factor in all our child welfare problems is the regular employment of the father at a reasonable wage" (Helen Keller newspaper series, May 27, 1931, Edith and Grace Abbott Papers, University of Chicago Library).

In a summation of her thoughts on this subject, Grace Abbott wrote in her book *From Relief to Social Security,* "Unemployment may be regarded—in greater or less degree—as the inevitable result of our industrial system. Our economic life is based upon it. A democracy which supports this system should, therefore, make adequate and democratic provision for its victims, recognizing the cost of their care as the price it pays for the continuance of the capitalist system. Certainly, those who profit most by this system should be the ones to insist that these costs be cheerfully met."

11. The Real American Vice

1. The Conference of State and Provincial Health Authorities of North America was an organization that brought together U.S. and Canadian public health officers and their allies. The U.S. members of the organization tried and failed to get a national health insurance provision included in the landmark 1935 Social Security Act.

2. Nathan Strauss was a wealthy New York businessman and partner in R. H. Macy & Company. As a philanthropist he was best known for building "milk stations" which distributed pure milk to poor families.

3. Dr. S. Josephine Baker (1873–1945) was the first female to hold the post of U.S. Assistant Surgeon General. Baker headed the Bureau of Child Hygiene in the U.S. Public Health Service.

4. The Association for Improving the Condition of the Poor was a national charity founded in the late nineteenth century that emphasized the need to establish children's medical clinics for impoverished youngsters. Together with school systems in large cities it distributed free lunches for needy children, establishing a model later integrated into such federal programs as the National School Lunch Program. The New York Outdoor Medical Clinic was founded in 1908 and focused on prenatal care for impoverished mothers.

5. During the 1930s when pediatrics emerged as a growing medical

specialty, the Maternity Center Association continued to advocate the importance of training midwives, making it one of the last organizations openly to challenge physicians' dominance in birthing rooms.

6. As late as the 1930s, American men still enjoyed longer lifespan averages than did women due to deaths connected to pregnancy and childbirth.

7. Dr. Earnest Caulfield and George Armstrong both helped establish pediatrics as a recognized medical field in the early twentieth century.

8. In 1899 Illinois enacted the first law creating a special "juvenile court" to deal exclusively with criminal and abused children. By 1930 all states, with the exception of Maine, had copied the precedent and organized separate courts for children in their cities and counties. In theory, if frequently not in reality, juvenile courts were protective and rehabilitative, not punitive—though young offenders who were sent to "detention centers" understandably still saw themselves as prisoners. Through the 1930s, and indeed after, no standard definition of "juvenile" or "juvenile delinquency" prevailed. Most juvenile courts reviewed cases involving individuals under age eighteen, though significant variations existed. Some courts dealt only with children accused of lawbreaking. Others adjudicated problems related to offenses committed by adults against children, such as desertion or physical molestation.

9. Progressive-era social welfare campaigns often spanned oceans and territorial borders. Both Grace and Edith Abbott embodied this international reform spirit.

12. The Washington Traffic Jam

1. The National Institute of Social Sciences was an organization founded in the late nineteenth century as new university-based disciplines such as sociology and anthropology emerged. The institute was an ardent supporter of Franklin D. Roosevelt's New Deal.

2. Homer Folks was a prominent progressive reformer, the founder of the Children's Aid Society, and a vocal crusader for restrictions on child labor.

3. The Department of Labor itself, not just the Children's Bureau, was an early-twentieth-century addition and ranked low on the cabinet-level totem pole. Though Frances Perkins served as a highly effective industrial commissioner in New York before following Franklin Roosevelt to Washington as the first female cabinet appointee, she faced a great deal of opposition, particularly from union leaders violently opposed to a woman serving as the head of the Department of Labor. In the 1930s and early 1940s the Department of Labor, under Perkins, repeatedly lost administrative turf

battles, almost 50 percent of its budget, and many of its agencies and bureaus. The Children's Bureau ended up in the new Federal Security Administration and was then later moved to the Department of Health, Education, and Welfare.

4. Opponents frequently, and incorrectly, saw "socialism," "communism," and "Russian influences" in the work of the Children's Bureau, which they consistently referred to as "this Socialist Bureau" or "a Socialist Propaganda agency." They also frequently damned the Children's Bureau as an advocate of the use of birth-control devices (still illegal at the time), such as condoms and diaphragms.

5. Grace Abbott's frustrations with the Washington scene resonate throughout her writings. She was especially concerned with the difficulties that were experienced in explaining both her work and the Bureau's needs to visiting politicians and dignitaries from around the world. In 1930 she wrote, "A great many visitors come to the U.S. to see what is being done for children. They come to the Children's Bureau and ask where they had better go, and I usually say, 'Well, do you want to see some of our best, or some of our worst?' They look surprised because I say there are any 'worst things' and I explain that right near Washington we can show them some of the worst things being done for children anywhere, as well as some of the very best. Well, they have really come to see the best, but it is the other that ought to interest us, for the things being badly done for children ought to be in the process of correction" (scaa [State Charities Aid Association] News, February 1930).

13. Why Did Child Labor Ever Develop in America?

1. Established in 1933 as an effort to fight the Great Depression, the National Recovery Administration (NRA) tried to stabilize wages and prices by creating codes of fair competition for hundreds of different industries, including the textile trades. Though the legislation authorizing the NRA demanded that workers, employers, and consumers all have seats on code-planning boards, in reality the Cotton Textile Codes were largely union-hostile industry creations. The U.S. Supreme Court declared the NRA unconstitutional in 1935.

2. Robert Owen (1771–1858) was a British Utopian reformer who was identified with advocating the establishment of model workers' communities.

3. Grace Abbott spoke and wrote on the importance of the anti–child labor movement innumerable times during her career. In her 1938 book, *The Child and the State*, she pointed out, "The child labor movement has in

every country supplied the shock troops in the struggle for decent working conditions. The victories secured in the early child labor laws opened the way for general regulation of factory conditions and demonstrated the necessity for a factory-inspection system. Child labor laws were also a pioneering effort on the part of the state to insure to children a national minimum standard, a recognition that large numbers of parents were unable—and a few unwilling—to give their children the protection which under the common law was their duty."

14. Promoting the Welfare of All Children

1. Lillian Wald (1867–1940) was an American reformer who was best known as a supporter of publicly funded health care and was instrumental in the creation of the Children's Bureau. Florence Kelley (1859–1932) was a champion of consumers' rights and restrictions on child labor, a settlement house advocate, and a civil rights crusader. She was connected with both Hull House and New York's Henry Street Settlement. Kelley and Wald organized the New York Child Labor Committee in 1902, and Kelley was a founder of the National Child Labor Committee in 1904 as well as the National Association for the Advancement of Colored People (NAACP) in 1909.

2. William Howard Taft was the twenty-seventh president of the United States from 1909 to 1913. The Children's Bureau was established during his term of office, although he was not a great champion of the agency.

3. "The Delectable Mountains" and "the Enchanted Mound" are allegorical nicknames found in *The Pilgrim's Progress* (1678) by John Bunyan, which is also the source of phrases such as "Vanity Fair" and "the House Beautiful." The Delectable Mountains and the Enchanted "Ground" (as it actually is) are landmark places along the journey to heaven pursued by the book's hero, Christian. Bunyan's book was a favorite reading choice of the Abbott household in Nebraska, and both Grace and Edith Abbott, throughout their lives, regularly used phrases from this book when making analogies or explaining ideas.

How Women Achieve in Government

1. Frances Perkins (1882–1965) was the U.S. Secretary of Labor from 1933 to 1945 under President Franklin D. Roosevelt. She was the first woman in U.S. history appointed to the presidential cabinet. Before her appointment as Secretary of Labor, she served as a member and as chairman of the New York State Industrial Board and as commissioner of the New York State Industrial Commission.

17. Women

1. Inez Haynes Irwin (1873–1970) was a Brazilian-born writer who worked as a correspondent in Europe during World War I. She also wrote fiction, an etiquette book for girls, and a travel book about California. *Angels and Amazons* (subtitled "A Hundred Years of American Women") was a collection of biographical sketches.

2. Sophonisba Breckinridge (1866–1948) was a social work educator, Hull House resident, and member of the Kentucky Bar. Breckinridge worked closely with Edith Abbott, both as faculty colleague at the University of Chicago's Graduate School of Social Service Administration (SSA) and as frequent coauthor. Breckinridge cofounded and edited the *Social Service Review*.

Bibliography

Abbott, Edith. "A Prairie Childhood." *Great Plains Quarterly* 23, no. 2 (Spring 2003): 93–110.

———. "A Sister's Memories." *Social Service Review* 13 (September 1939): 351–408.

Abbott, Othman A. *Recollections of a Pioneer Lawyer.* Lincoln: Nebraska Historical Society, 1928.

Abbott Papers, Abbott Sisters Research Center, Edith Abbott Memorial Library, Grand Island NE.

Addams, Jane. *The Second Twenty Years at Hull House: September 1909 to September 1929.* New York: Macmillan, 1930.

Bradbury, Dorothy. *Four Decades of Action for Children.* Washington DC: Children's Bureau, 1956.

The Child 4, no. 2 (1939). [Grace Abbott Tribute Issue.]

Costin, Lela. *Two Sisters for Social Justice.* Urbana: University of Illinois Press, 1983.

Edith and Grace Abbott Papers, 1870–1967, Joseph Regenstein Library, Special Collections Research Center, University of Chicago Library, Chicago IL.

Fitzpatrick, Ellen. *Endless Crusade.* Oxford: Oxford University Press, 1990.

Kirkland, Winifred. "Grace Abbott," in *Girls Who Became Leaders,* by Winifred and Frances Kirkland. New York: Long and Smith, 1932.

Lemons, J. Stanley. *The Woman Citizen, Social Feminism in the 1920s.* Urbana: University of Illinois Press, 1973.

Lifson, Amy. "Grace Abbott and the Struggle for Social Reform," *Humanities* 18, no. 1 (1997): 40–41.

Lindemeyer, Kriste. *A Right to Childhood: The U.S. Children's Bureau and Child Welfare, 1912–1946.* Urbana: University of Illinois Press, 1997.

Marks, Rachel. "Published Writings of Edith Abbott: A Bibliography," *Social Service Review* 32 (March 1958): 51–56.

Mink, Gwendolyn, and Rickie Solinger, eds. *Welfare: A Documentary History of U.S. Policy and Politics.* New York: New York University Press, 2003.

Muncy, Robin. *Creating a Female Dominion in American Reform, 1890–1935.* New York: Oxford University Press, 1991.

———. "Grace Abbott," *Women Building Chicago, 1790–1990: A Biographical Dictionary.* Ed. Rima Lunin Schultz and Adele Hast. Bloomington: Indiana University Press, 2001.

Smuts, Alice, and Robert Smuts. *Science in the Service of Children.* New Haven: Yale University Press, 2006.

Sorensen, John. *The Children's Champion.* Chicago Public Radio, WBEZ-FM, 2003.

———. *My Sister and Comrade.* Nebraska Public Radio, 1995.

Wisner, Elizabeth. "Edith Abbott's Contributions to Social Work Education," *Social Service Review* 32 (March 1958): 1–10.

Wright, Helen. "Three Against Time: Edith and Grace Abbott and Sophonisba P. Breckinridge," *Social Service Review* 28 (March 1954): 41–50.

Selected Works by Grace Abbott

"Accomplishments and a Challenge," *Public Health Nurse* 20 (December 1928).

"After Suffrage—Citizenship," *The Survey* 44 (September 1, 1920).

"The Chicago Employment Agency and Immigrant Worker," *American Journal of Sociology* 14 (November 1908).

The Child and the State. Chicago: University of Chicago Press, 1938.

"Child Labor Movement," *North American Magazine* 220 (December 1924).

"The Democracy of Internationalism," *The Survey* 36 (August 5, 1916).

"Developing Standards of Rural Child Welfare," in *Proceedings of the National Conference of Social Work.* University of Chicago Press, 1927.

"Federal Aid for the Protection of Maternity and Infancy," *American Journal of Sociology* 12 (August 1922).

"Federal Regulation of Child Labor 1906–38," *Social Service Review* 13 (September 1939).

From Relief to Social Security. Chicago: University of Chicago Press, 1941.

"Human Cost of Unemployment," *American Labor Legislation Review* 23 (March 1933).

The Immigrant and the Community. New York: The Century Company, 1917.

"May Day: Child Health Day, 1933," *Child Health Bulletin* 9 (May 1933).

"The Midwife in Chicago," *American Journal of Sociology* 20 (March 1915).

"Safeguarding the Child in America," *Current History* 33 (March 1931).

"Saving America's Children," *Current History Magazine of the New York Times* 17 (January 1923).

"A Study of the Greeks in Chicago," *American Journal of Sociology* 15 (October 1909).

"A Ten Year Child Welfare Plan," *Parent's Magazine* 7 (May 1932).

"Ten Years' Work for Children," *North American Magazine* 218 (August 1923).

"Time to Ratify," *Collier's* 99 (April 1937).

"Twenty Years of the Children's Bureau," *Social Service Review* 6 (March 1932).

"What About Mothers' Pensions Now?" *The Survey* 70 (March 1934).

"What to Expect of the White House Conference," *Parent's Magazine* 5 (October 1930).

To be interested in others and to want to help is the answer to those who seek to make their lives interesting and happy, as well as useful. Doing the next thing, and making good at it, has this certain advantage: You can never tell what it is going to lead to, or what new and possibly thrilling experience is lying in wait just around the corner.

—GRACE ABBOTT, July 31, 1926

Index

children (*continued*)
preparation for American citizenship, 11–15; public protection for,
43–49, 78–80; Sheppard-Towner
Maternity and Infancy Act and,
xvii–xviii, 34–36; and U.S.
Children's Bureau, ix, xiv–xix,
33–38
citizenship, American, 10–17, 46
Civil Service Commission, 97–98
community planning and immigrants,
18–24

democratic internationalism, 23–24
Democratic Party, 100
Dix, Dorothea, 87–93

education: of children, 43–44, 46–47;
government funding for public,
43–44, 48–49; of immigrants,
14–16, 19; of women, xi–xii, 83–84
Ellis Island, 9, 28
employment: of children and
adolescents, xv–xvii, 14–15,
27–29, 39–42, 53–56, 72–73; of
immigrants, 14–15, 21, 27–29
English instruction for immigrants,
14–16, 19

Federal Child Labor Law, 40, 53–54
Folks, Homer, 68
foster-home care, 57–58, 77–78
From Relief to Social Security (G. Abbott),
77, 117n1 (chap. 10)

General Federation of Women's Clubs,
91
government: bureaucracy, 68–71,
119n4; and public relief, 59–62;
reform, 43–49; and responsibility to
children, 116n2; treatment of the
mentally ill by, 87–89; women in,
83–86, 96–103. *See also* legislation

Great Depression, the, 77–80, 119n1

Hamilton, Alexander, 72–73, 113n2
(chap. 5)
Harding, Warren, 35, 61
health of immigrants, 21, 28–29. *See
also* public health
Hoover, Herbert, 50
Hull House, ix, xii, 3–6, 94, 120n1
(chap. 14), 121n2

The Immigrant and the Community (G.
Abbott), xiv
immigrant(s): adjustments during
first years in the U.S., 19–20;
assimilation of, 22–23; children
of, 11–15; communities in larger
cities, 20; community planning
and, 18–24; countries of origin,
xiii, 112n2 (chap. 3); at Ellis
Island, 9, 28; employment of, 21,
27–29; English instruction for,
14–16, 19; families, 11–15; health
of, 21, 28–29; at Hull House,
5–6; legislation affecting, 111n2,
115n5; poverty among, 25–30;
and preparation for American
citizenship, 10–17, 46; problems
of, 25–30; protection of, xiii–xiv;
public health and, 21; resentment
of, 22–23; as single mothers, 29–30;
travel and, 7–9
Immigrants' Protective League, ix, 3–4,
28–29, 111n1
infant mortality, 51–52
internationalism, democratic, 23–24
Irwin, Inez Haynes, 94–95, 121n1

Keating-Owen Law, xv–xvii
Kelley, Florence, 120n1 (chap. 14)

Lathrop, Julia, xii, xiv, 33, 64, 74, 85,
98